# AN INTRODUCTION TO

# CAT CARE

## DR MORAG KERR

# AN INTRODUCTION TO
# CAT CARE

## DR MORAG KERR

THE WELLFLEET PRESS

WELLFLEET

A QUINTET BOOK

This edition published 1990 by Wellfleet Press
110 Enterprise Avenue
Secaucus, New Jersey 07094

ISBN 1 55521 548 3

This book was designed and produced by
Quintet Publishing Limited
6 Blundell Street
London N7 9BH

Design Director: Peter Bridgewater
Art Director: Ian Hunt
Designer: Nicky Simmonds
Editor: Caroline Beattie
Picture Research: Michael Nicholson

Typeset in Great Britain by
Central Southern Typesetters, Eastbourne
Manufactured in Hong Kong by
Regent Publishing Services Limited
Printed in Hong Kong by
Leefung-Asco Printers Limited

# Contents

INTRODUCTION

# A New Member of the Household

▲ *While not essential, a little warm milk is appreciated by most kittens.*

A NEW MEMBER OF THE HOUSEHOLD

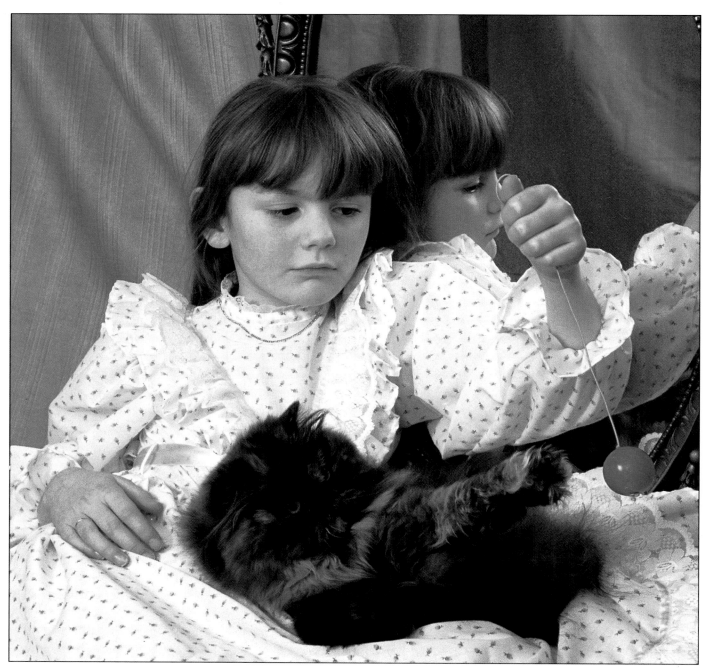

▲ *A little girl and her cat make a charming picture together.*

## WHY HAVE A PET?

There is a very special quality to our relationships with our pets, partly because we always see ourselves as the controlling partner (whether or not this is actually the case), and partly due to that special feeling of communication – two-way communication – with someone who is not human and is in many ways utterly alien, which none of our relationships with people can ever provide. The human/companion animal bond is a very special experience; many people will unbend and unburden themselves to their pets in a way which they never will to other people.

It can be particularly enriching for children, as they learn the responsibility of caring for someone totally dependent on them, and to relate to someone who cannot be won over by tantrums or sulks. Pets can also provide an introduction to the 'facts of life'.

For people suffering from stress and tension the mere act of stroking a pet will lower the blood pressure, slow the heart and promote a feeling of calm and well-being. Experience is showing that where confused elderly people and mentally handicapped people are concerned a pet can draw them out of their shells and encourage conversation in a way that nothing else will.

Pets are, basically, a good thing.

▲ *Cats have the gift of appearing at ease in any situation – high, low or anywhere in between.* ◄

## WHY HAVE A CAT?

Practically speaking, a pet fulfils the above requirements in a way that no other pet can, and there are a number of special reasons for choosing a cat. Many people are just natural cat lovers, and unless there is something of this in your character than a cat is probably not a good idea for you. However, there are many sane, logical reasons for having one: compared to dogs, for example, cats are relatively undemanding pets. In particular they do not need to be taken for walks and are much more amenable to being left alone in the house. This makes them particularly suitable for households where everyone is at work all day, or for people with restricted mobility. Cats are gentle, graceful, clean and cuddly, and often are less demanding of overt demonstrations of affection than dogs, being content with peaceful companionship. They are also masters and mistresses of the art of appearing aloof and independent, which has the effect of making their chosen humans feel especially privileged and favoured. To many people, the cat is the perfect pet.

## RESPONSIBILITIES TO YOUR CAT

To paraphrase a well-known saying, 'a cat is for life, not just for Christmas'. When you take on a cat you are accepting a new member into your family, one which will give you a great deal, but one which will be completely dependent on you for all of his or her life. It is almost like getting married – for better, for worse, for richer, for poorer, in sickness (the cat's or yours) or in health, until death do you part – and it is not a commitment to be entered into lightly or on a whim. He or she will need food, shelter, companionship and medical care, and will need them all the time, not just when it is convenient, or

▲ *A pair of kittens from the same litter will play together happily and keep each other amused, even when their humans are busy or absent.*

when you are (or are not) on holiday, or when you can afford it. Cats are not very expensive pets, but they do require money spent on them and you should realize that a cat costs more to feed than a dog of up to about Cocker Spaniel size. In the natural course of events most people will expect to outlive their cat, but things do not always go as expected and you should also think about providing for your cat in your will – consider who might be prepared to offer him or her a home, and consider a small legacy to help towards the cost of this.

## RESPONSIBILITIES TO OTHER PEOPLE

The world is not entirely peopled by cat-lovers, and you should realize that not everyone will find your pet totally

▶ *Cats naturally regard any part of the house as theirs for the occupying – so beware if you are coming downstairs with a loaded tray!*

and unreservedly adorable. One dog which is badly controlled is certainly more of a menace than ten cats, which is just as well, as there is a limit to what you can persuade a cat not to do (short of keeping him permanently indoors), but this does not relieve you of all responsibilities. Unneutered (entire) tomcats are a positive menace – they caterwaul half the night, and spray foul-smelling urine around their territory – and even if you can put up with this yourself it is not particularly considerate to other people.

Another point to think about with all cats is toilet

provision. If you have no garden a litter tray is essential, and if this is left outside it must be positioned considerately and cleaned and tidied regularly. If you share a garden, consider whether your neighbours might object to your cat digging up the flower bed, and, again, think about a well-sited litter tray. Remember also that some people are allergic to cats and be prepared to keep your cat well away if a visitor is so troubled. Finally, think about public health. It is not only necessary to keep your cat free of parasites and infectious diseases for the cat's sake and your own, but also for the sake of other cats and

people with whom he might come into contact. This is one reason for the importance of a regular health-care programme.

## DRAWBACKS AND DANGERS OF CAT OWNING

Everybody knows that cats are clean, but perhaps they are not quite as clean as all that. They shed hair (light hair, which is selectively attracted to dark objects, and dark hair, which is . . . well, that is how it seems). They trail

A NEW MEMBER OF THE HOUSEHOLD

▲ *A cat owner is always assured of a welcome home. Of course, the empty food bowl may have something to do with this!*

mud indoors. They can be messy eaters and distribute cat food liberally about the kitchen. Some cats develop bad habits of clawing furniture or spraying urine indoors, and, of course, they are a physical tie and responsibility. If you are excessively houseproud, perhaps a tank of tropical fish would suit you better.

There are also quite genuine dangers. Cats come armed at all corners, their claws are sharp and they can inflict a very nasty bite. Not all cats are perfectly safe with babies or toddlers. And while there are many, many diseases you can catch from other people compared to only a few from cats, these few should be considered. The most important are toxoplasma (cross-infection is rare but the consequences are serious enough that pregnant women should never handle a cat's litter tray), toxocara (round-worms, which can cross-infect humans with their larval stages, but which are far less likely to be a problem with cats than with dogs) and ringworm (which cats can sometimes carry without showing signs of infection). These problems and their control are discussed later in the book. However, it is *not* true that you can catch AIDS from cats.

## THE FINAL VERDICT

If all these drawbacks have failed to dissuade you, then you are probably ready for the joys and exasperations of cat-owning. This book aims to give you a basic guide to how to go about this, and is written with the first-time owner particularly in mind.

## CHAPTER ONE

# Acquiring
# Your Cat

▲ *Some crosses produce very attractive results.*

ACQUIRING YOUR CAT

## TYPE OF CAT

Probably only a minority of cat-owners actually get any choice as to what type of cat they adopt. Many people have no real intention of having a cat at all, until they have been persuaded by a friend with a litter of kittens, or simply wake up one day to find that they are sharing their home with a four-legged free-loader. Still, assuming that you have not already succumbed to the blandishments of a furry charmer with a plausible sob-story, you can allow yourself the illusion of free will by considering what type of cat you might prefer. Of course, once your future cat decides that you are the human he prefers, your opinion is unlikely to count for much!

■ **LONGHAIR OR SHORTHAIR?** In cats, the gene for long hair is recessive to that for short hair, and so most non-pedigree cats are shorthairs. Their sleek coats are undoubtedly very handsome, and when a shorthair has intricate markings such as one of the types of tabby pattern, the sharp definition of the markings is often extremely smart. However, it must be admitted that there is something particularly attractive about the longhair, and a long plumed tail and perfect chocolate box face have charmed their way into many a household.

Before you decide on a longhair, however, you should consider whether or not you want to take on the amount of grooming involved. The average non-pedigree longhair, or the medium longhair breeds such as the Birman or the Maine Coon, are perhaps not too much of a bother as one really thorough grooming session a week is usually sufficient to meet health considerations, but the extremely longhaired breeds of the Persian type do involve a great deal of work. Thorough daily combing is absolutely essential in these breeds to prevent the serious problems which will arise if the cat's coat is allowed to become matted. For this reason the smart, easy-care shorthair is usually the better choice for a busy household.

■ **PEDIGREE OR NON-PEDIGREE?** The lack of a written documentation of the precise ancestry has never prevented a cat from considering himself an aristocrat, or from behaving like one. In view of this, there are probably only two reasons for having a definite preference for a pedigree cat: if you would prefer to know fairly precisely how your little bundle of fluff will look in six months' time, especially if you have formed a particular liking for the appearance or character of a specific breed; or if you are interested in breeding or showing pedigree cats. Another reason may be the suggestion that people who

▶ *Bright-eyed and alert, these kittens are almost ready to venture out into the world. Even at this early age it is clear that they are longhairs.*

14

▲ *This aristocratic lady, a silver tortoiseshell longhair, is in fact a non-pedigree.*

are allergic to cats may be able to tolerate the Rex breeds, with their fine wavy coats, but you should realize that this is not invariably the case, and a number of sufferers who have bought Rex kittens have found the problem unabated.

Much concern is often expressed about certain dog breeds being inherently unsound or suffering from inherited diseases, but fortunately the pedigree cat world is in a much better state. There are a few breeds with genes which veterinary surgeons would class as 'deformities' – the Rex coat (Cornish or Devon), the tail-less Manx, the hairless Sphinx and the folded ears of the Scottish Fold. However, of these only the old-established Manx gene is associated with any truly serious health problems, and these are matters which mainly concern breeders, as the nature of the problem is such that Manx kittens which are actually born healthy are not really any more likely that any other cat to run into trouble at a later age. The other main area of concern is the flat, Pekingese-type face encouraged by breeders of the Persian-type longhairs and colourpoints. These cats are probably more likely than average to develop nose and respiratory problems, but the head shape is not nearly so exaggerated as with the dogs and so long as the breeders maintain a sense of proportion the cats may stay free of the really serious side-effects such as ulceration of the cornea of the eye.

If your preference does lie for a pedigree cat, you should try to find out as much as possible about your chosen breed in advance, and preferably get in touch with one of the breed societies for the breed in question. This will put you in a much better position to judge what you want when you come to choose a kitten, and the breed society may be able to put you in touch with breeders with litters ready for homing at the time you require.

If you choose a non-pedigree, do not be ashamed of his lack of paper lineage. 'Domestic short (or long) hair', the correct description of a non-pedigree cat, does not mean he is a mongrel or cross-bred, as these cats usually have no ancestors at all of official breeding, but came from a line no less distinguished in its own local way. Many people will actually prefer the natural appearance of a cat whose genes have not been hothouse-bred for the show ring. You should also note that the lack of a pedigree is no barrier to showing a cat – many shows have a special household pet (non-pedigree) section where competition can be just as intense (and as catty) as in the pedigree section! The compromise position, choosing a half-pedigree or part-pedigree cat, is also available, and such mixtures can produce some extremely attractive animals.

■ **ADULT OR KITTEN?** There are few things more attractive than an eight-week old bundle of fluff, all huge eyes and uncertain paws, doing cute kittenish things with a ball of wool. If your circumstances permit it, you really ought not to deprive yourself of this uniquely charming stage in your cat's life. However, kittens need a great deal more attention than adult cats, and it is extremely unfair to leave an inquisitive, playful kitten shut up alone in the house all day. Quite apart from the effect on the kitten's social development, the cute kittenish things he will almost certainly begin to do to the upholstery and curtains will be much less cute, and cause much more damage, when a 10- or 12-pound cat does them, and habits once formed can be difficult to break. One way round the isolation problem is to adopt two kittens from the same litter, always assuming you can cope with bedlam twice over.

A more suitable solution for situations where the cat will have to be left alone for long periods of the day may be to offer a home to an adult. There is never any shortage of adult cats looking for a friendly home, and these animals are often comparatively placid and undemanding, and much happier to settle down to sleep while you are absent from the house. Being older, they may need a little more concentrated tact and bribery for the first few days and the full relationship may take longer to develop, but they often do the initial settling in more quickly than active, inquisitive kittens. There is no doubt that adult cats are capable of forming extremely strong and lasting bonds of affection with owners who in many cases are treating them better than they have ever been treated before. If you would like a cat, but due to age, disability or the need to go out to earn the price of the cat food you feel unable to cope with a kitten, then you are probably the answer to an older cat's prayer.

## FINDING A CAT

■ **BREEDERS** If you have decided on a pedigree cat, then a specialist breeder is undoubtedly the best source. Breeders can be contacted through breed societies, through advertisements in weekly or monthly cat magazines, or even by direct approach at shows. When you approach a breeder, make sure you are clear whether you simply want a pedigree pet, or whether you are yourself interested in showing or breeding. A potential show winner or stud cat will obviously be much more expensive than one of pet quality, and you should do your best to find out what points to look for in such an animal, or take along a knowledgeable friend, to be certain you get what you are paying for. However, most breeders know what sort of a home they want for each kitten, and if you are open about your requirements and intentions they will match you up with a suitable youngster.

If your preference is for an adult pedigree, breeders are again good people to approach. Such cats do become available for a variety of reasons – a breeder with a full house may prefer to re-home an adult neuter, for example

ACQUIRING YOUR CAT

– and if you make your desire known then a little shake of the grapevine may produce just the cat for you.

■ **PET SHOPS.** Nowadays, few pet shops sell puppies or kittens, preferring to confine their attention to fish, small rodents and pet supplies. It is certainly not a good idea to acquire a pedigree animal in a pet shop, or at least not if you actually want to be sure of its pedigree, but you may want to consider them regarding non-pedigrees. The usual pet-shop environment does increase the risk of infectious disease well above that of a private home, but no more so than the environment of the RSPCA, ASPCA or other animal-rescue charity, and the general unsuitability of pet-shop accommodation for more than a very short-term stay means that kittens or cats in such an establishment may be in nearly as much need of rescue as the charity home inmates.

■ **CAT RESCUE SOCIETIES.** It is a sad reflection of our attitude to the cat that in nearly every town you will find at least one such charity organization whose members spend a lot of time searching desperately for homes for their lost and abandoned charges. If you are looking for a non-pedigree, particularly if you are considering an adult cat, this is certainly the place to look. The best societies will not only be able to tell you each cat's history as far as they know it but they will describe to you the cat's habits, character, likes and dislikes and generally be in an excellent position to help you assess which cat is the most likely to suit your personality. Of course, what usually happens is that you look at one particular cat, he looks at you, and that is that. Good rescue societies will also make sure that all the cats they home are neutered and vaccinated at least against feline infectious enteritis, and will of course appreciate a donation to cover the costs of this.

It is always a moral dilemma as to whether to go to a home with a policy of putting cats to sleep after a certain length of stay. Such establishments usually do not neuter or vaccinate either. There is always the feeling that one should not support a 'rescue' home with such a policy, but their cats are arguably even more in need of a home than those in the permanent rescue sanctuaries.

■ **PRIVATE HOMES.** These are an excellent source of non-pedigree kittens, and if you do not happen to have a friend whose cat has had a litter, the columns of the local paper will nearly always yield a list of advertisements of the 'free to good home' variety. When responding to such an advertisement, make the most of your opportunity to meet the mother (and perhaps even the father) as this will give you at least some idea of the likely character and

▶ *A family group of Somalis, the semi-longhair variant of the Abyssinian breed.*

▲ *Cat sanctuary life may be a little crowded at times, but the inmates are safe, cared-for and well fed.*

▶ *Is this cat sizing up the accommodation before deciding to take over a new home?*

appearance of their offspring. If you want to avoid taking on a kitten with health problems, check that the mother is not underweight or suffering from any visible signs of disease such as fleas, ear mites or runny eyes/nose, that the kittens are plump and appear contented, and that the general environment of the brood is clean and well-organized. Kittens should be at least eight weeks old and weaned on to solid food before they leave their mother, so if yours is not yet at that stage then be prepared to be patient and wait until he is ready before you bring him home.

■ **BEING ADOPTED BY A CAT.** In a large number of cases it is the cat who does the adopting, simply walking in to a chosen home and settling in. This is fine, so far as it goes, and it does give you at least the nominal option of saying no if you feel you are not compatible (though if the cat is determined, you are almost certainly a lost cause). However, you should consider the possibility that your Ginger is somebody else's Kitty, and try to make sure you are not the victim of a cat's two-timing scheme before you let him move in. There have been a number of very unpleasant incidents, some resulting in court cases, which have arisen

from two families feeling they had equal, exclusive claims to one cat. If you are adopted by a cat, buy a collar and a 'message capsule' type name tag for the cat, and enclose a message with your name, address, telephone number and the statement that this cat wishes to adopt you, and anyone with any objections should contact you as soon as possible. If there has been no response within a week or two you have acquired a cat.

## THE FINAL CHOICE

■ **PICKING OUT YOUR CAT OR KITTEN.** When selecting a kitten from a litter, or an adult cat from a rescue society, there are a few general points which can help you choose. You should try to find a confident, outgoing sort of cat, as these usually make the best pets – the kitten who comes forward to investigate your shoes or the adult who allows you to approach rather than scampering to hide in a corner are the ones to note. You should also feel that the cat or kitten is comfortable in your arms and does not resent being picked up or held, but realize that there is a difference between the clawing panic of a really shy, un-

social cat, and the fairly polite wriggle that says 'Not so fast – I hardly know you!' It is always gratifying if the cat begins to purr and rubs his head affectionately on your chest, but do not think badly of him if he does not – cats who are not immediately ready to throw themselves at any stranger often make the most loyal, attached pets once they are settled.

Consider also health matters. Look for a sleek, clean, cared-for coat, bright alert eyes with no discharges and no sign of third-eyelid protrusion, and clean ears. Gummy eyes and/or nose usually signal an infection which you would do well to avoid. To check whether a cat is too thin, feel his back for very sharp, protruding edges of the bones of the spine. A thin cat with a 'pot-bellied' appearance is a particularly bad risk. Of course, this is the time to let your heart rule your head, and when you fall in love with one particular cat you will find yourself ignoring every rule ever written. However, if you do decide to take on a potential problem cat, try to be sure that you understand what is involved and that you can cope before you make the final decision.

## PREPARING FOR THE NEW ARRIVAL

Before you bring your cat or kitten home, there are a few points you will consider. First, timing. Christmas is an extremely bad time to introduce a pet to a new home, especially where children are involved, and it is best to postpone things until after the New Year. Apart from this, try to arrange the arrival when you will have a fair amount of spare time to devote to helping him settle in. If the cat is eventually to be left alone all day, it is particularly important to allow the maximum time before he is left for the first time.

Before he arrives, you will also have to make a few decisions as to how you are going to manage the various necessities discussed in greater detail in Chapter 2, and then purchase the essential items. A provisional shopping list might read: food/water bowl set, plastic place mat, cat/kitten food, cat treats (dry cat food), cat bed, litter tray (preferably two), scoop and cat litter, collar and name tag, brush (and comb for a longhair), one or two toys, a scratching post, and a suitable cat carrier. These need not prove particularly expensive, and a number of items can be improvised.

■ **INTRODUCING THE CAT TO YOUR HOME.** By this time you should have finalized such momentous decisions as where he will sleep, which parts of the house will be out of bounds, and where the litter tray is to go. If you start as

*◄ A family of six Oriental Tabby kittens, almost ready to move to their new homes. Choosing just one of these charmers could be a real problem!*

you hope to go on this will give you an edge if it comes to any disagreement about these matters. Therefore, before you open the smart new cat carrier (cat carry-all), make sure the appropriate doors are shut (or open), and everything is arranged as you want it. Make sure also that the place is safe: no wobbly shelves, interesting boxes with poisonous contents or dangerous electrical fittings. Take particular care to ensure that high windows and balconies are closed or infallibly out of bounds. The first thing any cat will do in this circumstance is start to explore, and you know what curiosity did! The provision of a meal will probably help an older cat settle down, but a young cat may well ignore food until he has explored every inch of the new territory. It is better not to try to force your attention on him; instruct children not to grab. However, a frightened or insecure cat may need special petting, and if it does seem that the whole thing is a bit much, you may prefer to confine him to one room initially and gradually extend the bounds over a few days. When the cat seems ready, give him a good-sized meal, and do not disturb him if he settles down to sleep – particularly if he has chosen the correct spot! When it is time for bed, speak reassuringly when you turn out the light, but be firm about confining him in the area where *you* want him to sleep. It is natural for a cat to be unsettled at first, especially a kitten who has just left its mother, but he will settle happily after a night or two.

Over the next few days try to spend as much time as you can with the cat. Young cats will certainly enjoy lots of active play, and you will be tired out long before they are, but if an older cat is less active, or even seems a little standoffish, do not underestimate the importance of this period of togetherness in building up a bond of companionship. With this type of character, too much petting may be counterproductive at first, but a bit of judicious bribery with cat treats will often work wonders.

You should confine your new cat indoors for several days, to give him time to get used to the idea that you are the food provider and the person to come back to. A kitten will require more time than a cat, and it is also wise with a kitten to delay until after the vaccinations are complete. You will know how soon you can let him out by how settled he seems, but you should be sure he is comfortable with the new collar and name tag first, so that neighbours do not mistake him for a stray; if things go wrong anyone who finds him will be able to contact you easily. At first, accompany him on short trips just before feeding time, and be ready to snatch him back indoors if things start to get out of hand. If you think he is likely to

▶ *This terrarium is PROBABLY too heavy for the longhaired tabby kitten to push over – but it would be better not to take the risk.*

## HEALTH CHECK

**1** The mouth is checked for gum disease, tartar, and for loose or decaying teeth.

**2** Examining the eyes may reveal inflammation or discharges, and is also useful to check for anaemia.

**3** The weight check: bones should not feel sharp nor covered by fat.

**4** The ears should be clean and free from any signs of ear mite infestation.

**5** Palpation of the abdomen is important to check for lumps or pregnancy.

**6** It is important to check the cat's sex, although neutering is only obvious in males.

leap onto the wall and vanish, you may prefer to start with a harness and then to supervise the first few forays from the other end of a flexi-lead (flexible leash), at least until he is familiar enough with your garden to know where to return to. Remember, you can never force a cat to stay against his will, but if you have made the home comfortable, and he knows where it is, he will come back to you.

### THE FIRST VISIT TO THE VET

With a new kitten an early visit to the veterinary surgeon (veterinarian) for the first vaccinations is essential, but even when you are adopting an older cat who may already be vaccinated it is an excellent idea to arrange a health check. You will be given general advice about cat care, feeding, parasite control, neutering and so on, and so it is best to arrange this visit as soon as possible. However, a kitten cannot be given the first vaccinations until he is eight weeks old, so if he seems generally healthy there is probably little point in going earlier.

■ **CHOOSING A VET.** It is important to realize that once you have consulted a vet you are then his or her client, and it is contrary to professional ethics for another vet to take you on thereafter without informing the first vet and

arranging for any necessary transfer of medical records. This is not a particular problem if you are moving, or even if you simply want to change vets for some reason, but it does prevent casual 'shopping around' and means that you really should have your mind made up before you take your cat in for the first time. In some things there is no difference between practices – all vets must be fully qualified and registered, and in some countries all practices must provide a full 24-hour emergency service (though you should realize that except where a night deputizing service is utilized – rare outside large cities – this does mean waking a vet who has done a full day's work and has another to do tomorrow). You should, however, check that your chosen practice, or at least one of its members, does concentrate on small animal work, and that you are not just a side-line for an agricultural practice. Another point concerns the size of the practice. Large practices with several vets usually have a wider range of specialist equipment and facilities, but you may prefer the more personal attention of a small practice where there is a good chance of seeing the same vet on two consecutive occasions. Advertisements can provide some information, but you should try to find a pet-owning friend who can give you a personal recommendation, and the final choice is best made after a visit (without cat)

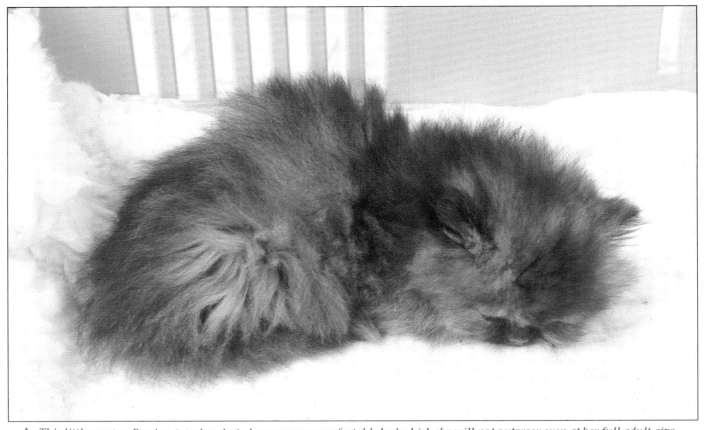

▲ *This little scrap, a Persian-type longhair, has a secure, comfortable bed which she will not outgrow even at her full adult size.*

▲ *If children and kittens are to grow up happily together it is important to teach the children to handle the kittens gently and to entice them into games rather than chasing or forcing them.*

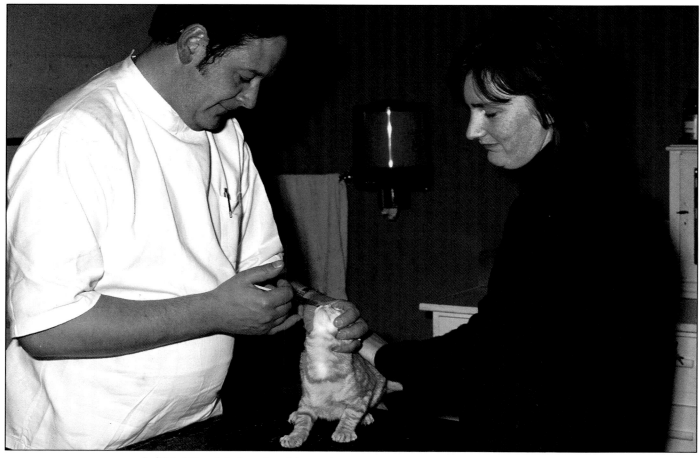

▲ *This kitten is being given his vaccination against cat flu by the intranasal route.*

to the surgery. Enquire about surgery (office) hours and such-like, and consider whether you feel that the staff are friendly and helpful, and you are generally comfortable with the practice.

■ **VACCINATIONS.** The two main feline diseases which your cat requires vaccination against are feline infectious enteritis (FIE, also known as panleucopenia) and cat flu. In countries where rabies occurs, rabies vaccination is also essential. FIE vaccination requires one injection at the minimum age of eight weeks, followed by a booster every year or two depending on your own vet's particular practice. This is probably the most vital vaccination, as although FIE is not actually very common it carries an extremely high mortality rate and very few cats survive it. Cat flu vaccination involves a primary course of two injections one month apart, again beginning no earlier than eight weeks, and this must be boosted every year. Cat flu is a much less serious illness than FIE, but it can be dangerous to young kittens and elderly cats, and infection is commonly passed on wherever cats mix in boarding catteries or at shows, for example. You will find that all good catteries insist on up-to-date cat flu (and FIE) vaccination before accepting cats, and so it is best to make sure this is done if there is any chance of your cat

having to go to a boarding cattery, especially at short notice. A vaccine against feline leukaemia virus (FeLV) has recently been developed which at the moment is only available in the USA, not in the UK. Your vet will be able to advise you about this and explain the precise vaccination regime against each disease, which will take into account the local prevalence of different types of infection.

■ **WORMING.** There are two main types of worms which affect cats: roundworms and tapeworms. The former are common in kittens as the infection is passed on in the mother's milk, while the latter are mainly picked up by hunting cats which eat mice, an intermediate host (though fleas are also implicated here), and so occur mainly in adults. Roundworms may also be contracted from mice or directly from other cats. A variety of different drugs are available to treat these parasites, some of which are effective against both types of worm. It is best to ask your vet about this at your first visit, and follow the advice given, which will be specific to your cat's age and lifestyle. Worming preparations are available at pet shops and chemists (drug stores), but the most effective drugs are the prescription-only ones which your vet can provide, and you will often find that as well as avoiding the risk of

ACQUIRING YOUR CAT

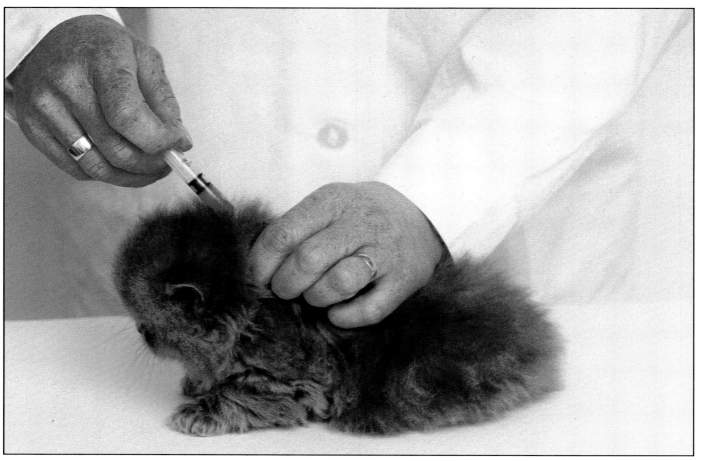

▲ *However, vaccination against feline infectious enteritis still requires a needle prick – usually into the skin of the neck.*

treating the wrong type of worms, the plainly packaged, non-catnip flavoured preparations from the vet are cheaper than the brands on sale over the counter.

■ **ECTOPARASITES.** This word refers to parasites which live on an animal's skin, which so far as cats are concerned means mainly fleas, and to a certain extent ear mites.

It is not true that all cats have fleas, but all cats are liable to catch them, however clean their household. Constant vigilance and a regular eradication strategy are essential, but nowadays fleas are quite easily dealt with, and you should not feel that the end of the world has arrived or that you are contaminated forever just because your pet has picked up a few unwanted guests. Again, the prescription treatments from your vet are much more effective than pet shop products, and even if your pet is passed as clear at the first visit it is worthwhile enquiring about this for future reference, and discussing the flea control strategy which will be most suitable for your circumstances.

Ear mites are also a common problem in cats, characterized by ear scratching and the presence of dark gritty wax in the ear. If any sign of these is seen during the health check, your vet will prescribe ear drops which generally clear the condition in about a week.

■ **NEUTERING AND CONTRACEPTION.** Although a kitten will not be old enough to be neutered until about five months of age, it is never too early to give the matter your consideration and you should discuss it with your vet at the earliest opportunity. If you have acquired an entire adult cat then this is a matter of some urgency.

An entire tomcat is completely unsuitable as a household pet. Tomcat urine has an amazingly unpleasant, pungent smell, and it is sprayed liberally on any available surface (in or out of doors) as a territory marker. This behaviour is virtually impossible to curb completely once it is established. Toms also have an almost uncontrollable urge to roam the countryside seeking queens on heat, and this inevitably results in violent fighting between rivals. Older toms often become badly beaten up in such encounters and bite abscesses are a common hazard. Neutered toms, on the contrary, make excellent pets with few undesirable habits and a more stay-at-home disposition. Even when a tom is adult the neutering operation usually produces excellent results, with the smell vanishing at once and the rakish habits gradually losing their grip, but it is best to have male kittens neutered before the spraying behaviour becomes established.

You should not allow feelings of 'he has a right to his natural behaviour' to influence you in this. Castration does not *force* a cat to behave differently, it removes the *desire* (indeed, compulsion) to carry out certain behavioural patterns. Cats are not sophisticated enough to perceive themselves as missing out on something they just do not want to do, and reasonably close observation will reveal that it is the stay-at-home neuters who in fact appear more contented, especially in later life. Even cat breeders, who usually keep their stud toms in a run in the garden, often have them fixed in middle age and see this as a kindness to the cats. Your vet will tell you that the operation is probably the simplest he or she ever has to perform. While there is always an element of risk whenever a general anaesthetic is involved complications are extremely rare and an overnight stay in hospital is seldom necessary.

While it is possible to keep an entire female cat (queen) as a household pet, again there are strong reasons for considering neutering. Queens come on heat (or call, after the vociferous yells of 'come and get me' which accompany the process) about every three weeks, often all year round when living indoors with artificial light. This is very trying for both cat and owner, as apart from the yelling, there is a lot of erotic rolling around on the carpet (which inexperienced owners sometimes mistake for evidence of severe pain), the inconvenience (for you), the smell and noise of half-a-dozen tomcats laying

siege to the house, and the frustration (for her) of not being able to carry the process to its natural conclusion (assuming you are successful in thwarting her attempts to get out to join the army of suitors under the window).

Under natural conditions a queen would be mated soon after the onset of call, which will then terminate naturally within a couple of days at the most. She would then not call again until after the kittens were weaned. Unmated, however, she may continue to call for up to 12 days, and may begin the whole process again only a week later. It has been known for some queens to call continuously for as long as three months, especially Siamese. This whole process can be extremely wearying for the owner, and it is fairly certain that the cat herself does not find it much fun after the first day or two. It is certainly not natural, and the only really practical alternative to the 'natural' situation (which is a litter of kittens twice or three times a year) is neutering. This operation, known as spaying, is more complex than castration as it involves incision into the abdominal cavity to remove ovaries and uterus, but again your vet will consider it a simple procedure and complications are very uncommon. It is, however, best not to proceed while the queen is calling, as there is an increased danger of haemorrhage.

Contraceptives are available for female cats, either by mouth or injection, and may be given either to prevent

## KITTENS AND ROUNDWORM

Ascarid roundworms grow in the intestines of a cat (**1**) and feed on the digested food there. Their eggs (**2**) are passed on via faeces, which may be swallowed by another cat, and if this happens, the larvae hatch in its intestines. The danger to a newborn kitten is that the larval stage of the *Toxocara cati* species migrate to the mother's milk at the onset of lactation and infect the kitten (**3**). Alternatively, the eggs of either of the known species of roundworm, *Toxocara cati* or *Toxocascaris leonina*, in the faeces may be eaten by another animal – such as a beetle, bird, rat or mouse (**4**) – that a cat may prey upon and so in turn infect the cat.

▲ *A bleeding ulcer like this should not be neglected – it could be a tumour in its early stages, which may be curable if treated in time.*

heat or to suppress it if a queen has started to call. However, these are generally used only where a queen is definitely intended for breeding (at a later date) and are not recommended for long-term use as a substitute for spaying. A 'morning after' injection is also available if your queen has defeated your efforts and escaped while on call, and must be given within 48 hours of mating. However, the drug can occasionally have serious side-effects and is only used for genuine accidents. There is little point in considering male contraception for cats, as the avoidance of kittens (usually somebody else's problem in any case) is the least of the worries of the owner of a pet tom, and measures such as vasectomy will do nothing to check the smell, spraying, roaming or fighting.

■ **DENTAL CARE.** The incidence of dental trouble in cats is extremely high, but the problem is not usually tooth decay but gingivitis (inflammation of the gums around the margins of the molar teeth) and/or tartar (which can build up in enormous quantities, again mostly on the outsides of the molars). Even quite young kittens often show evidence of the early stages at their first examination. There is always a dilemma as to just how far one should go in treating these conditions. Effective treatment usually requires a general anaesthetic in order to clean the tartar away (using an ultrasonic de-scaling machine) followed

by a course of antibiotics, possibly also with corticosteroids. These are powerful drugs, and repeated general anaesthetics must be considered to be risky. Your vet will therefore not want to leap in every time your cat's gums look a little red. The usual compromise is to leave all alone so long as his appetite is good and he shows no evidence of discomfort either while eating (indecision and making several attempts to pick up a piece of food) or at rest (sharp, jerky chewing motions made for no apparent reason), unless an extremely heavy buildup of tartar is seen at a routine examination. Ask your vet to show you how to check your cat's teeth (by pulling the side of the upper lip upwards and backwards) and keep a regular eye on the situation yourself. This will make it much easier to decide whether a sudden loss of appetite is due to a truly worsening dental situation, or whether some other cause is more likely. The feeding of occasional meals of dry (hard) cat food or the provision of a hard chew toy has been suggested as a means of exercising the teeth and slowing the buildup of tartar, but many owners find that this makes little difference. Some people do try to clean their cat's teeth either with a soft brush or a rag, using baking soda (sodium bicarbonate) as toothpaste. However, it is a rare cat indeed who will allow enough of this to make much difference, and if you persist too forcibly you make yourself an enemy for life!

**CHAPTER TWO**

# Caring for
# Your Cat

▲ *A selection of food available for cats: fresh, tinned and dry, with which it is important always to serve fresh water.*

▲ *Feeding time helps to enrich the relationship between you and your cat.*

*The quickest way to a cat's heart is through his stomach – but will this delicacy meet with his lordship's approval?*

## FEEDING

Cats require particularly careful feeding because of their rather unusual metabolism. They are what is known as obligate carnivores which means that they require as dietary essentials some factors which can only be found in animal tissues, and can therefore not live on a vegetarian diet. In the wild their full dietary needs are met by consuming all or most of the carcases of their prey, not just the meat, and in domestic surroundings it is necessary to mimic this by compounding the diet to include all these essential ingredients.

■ **PROPRIETARY CAT FOOD.** There is a feeling among some cat-owners that proprietary cat foods are in some way inferior to, or a poor substitute for fresh food, but in fact, so far as the leading brands are concerned, nothing could be further from the truth. Feline nutrition is a well-studied science, and the foremost investigators in the field have been the large pet-food manufacturers. They study both the optimum composition of the diet for long-term cat health and the maximum palatability of the food, and incorporate their findings in their products. The feeding of reputable brands of cat food therefore provides the quickest and easiest way to ensure that all the complex dietary needs of your pet are taken care of, usually in a tasty and attractive presentation. In fact the easy use of these products probably has had more influence than any other single factor in the growth of urban pet-keeping over the past few decades. Dog food, not being formulated with the cat's special needs in mind, is not suitable for feeding to cats.

There are three basic presentations of cat food – canned, semi-moist (in sealed plastic packets) and dry – with canned food probably being the most popular and the meat and jelly varieties generally proving more palatable than the meat and cereal ones. Semi-moist and dry foods have the advantages of being less messy, even easier to prepare (no can-opener!), and of being less liable to spoil in hot weather once opened. However, their comparative lack of variety makes them less suitable for use as an exclusive diet. The implication of dry cat food some years ago in the development of bladder trouble in male cats, although the problem has been generally rectified, has led to most manufacturers advising these types of food as occasional treats only. Many cats seem passionately fond of these products when fed in this way.

Variety is the golden rule when catering for your cat. Unlike dogs, cats become tired of eating the same food day in and day out, and often begin to refuse a once-loved

▲ *A front-opening wicker basket is probably the commonest type of cat carrier. A really determined cat could escape from this, but an extra two or three straps would make it more secure.*

product if it is fed monotonously. This variety can be achieved by utilizing the canned products of more than one manufacturer, by feeding occasional meals of semi-moist or dry food, and by switching between the different varieties available in the leading brands. Your cat will soon let you know his particular likes and dislikes, and you should pay attention to these to a reasonable extent but avoid indulging him excessively. There is little point in persevering with a food which your cat simply refuses to touch – pet cats are capable of starving themselves if they really detest what is offered (although feral cats will scavenge when they have to) – but if you give in to the

extent of never serving anything but his number one food you will be creating a tyrant. There is nothing more difficult to feed than a cat who is tired of his favourite but will not fancy anything else!

The amount of food is seldom a problem as most cats, given free access to food, do not tend to overeat and become fat. As a general guide a small queen may eat only half a 40-oz (400-g) can a day while a chunky tom may consume a whole can. Pregnant and nursing queens will of course require much more than this. As cats require much more protein than dogs it is not usual to feed meal or biscuit with canned food as is done with dogs – the canned food is complete in itself. The best guide is your cat's weight and general figure, and if an adult is maintaining a constant weight and appears neither fat nor thin then all is probably well. You should just be able to feel his ribs and spinal bones but without the bones feeling sharp. If you want to check his weight directly the easiest way is to weigh yourself, then pick up the cat and repeat the weighing – the difference is the cat's weight. If your cat is becoming round and is gaining weight you will have to harden your heart and restrict the amount of food you give, but if you think weight gain is something more sinister than just the result of greed, or if he is thin, losing weight and unwilling to increase his intake, then you ought to consult your veterinary surgeon.

However frequently you feed your cat, you will probably find that in the absence of competition he consumes the food in many small nibbles throughout the day. This is quite natural, and feline gobblers usually acquire that habit by bitter experience of seeing the food vanish rather than natural inclination. Two or three feeds a day are reasonable for an adult cat, but so long as you ensure that food is not lying around long enough to become rancid and the cat has a reasonable opportunity to consume his daily requirements, the actual timings are not very important. Cats are known to prefer their food at 98·4°F (37°C), but to warm it specially is probably carrying indulgence to excess. They will not eat hot food until it has cooled to about that temperature, and often leave refrigerated food until the chill has abated – this latter is a useful ploy to dampen the ardour of a greedy cat.

■ **FRESH FOOD.** This is inconvenient to prepare, requiring either daily shopping trips or lengthy defrosting; if fed as a sole diet needs great care to ensure it is balanced for those feline essentials mentioned earlier. It is also questionable whether such a diet really does work out cheaper than proprietary foods in the long run. However, occasional meals of fresh food can provide welcome variety for your cat. It is most important to ensure that meat, fish, eggs, rice, potatoes, etc. are *lightly* cooked before feeding to prevent food poisoning and the spread of parasites, improve digestibility and destroy certain undesirable substances in some of these foods. Ensure also that there are no sharp bones in the food. Variety in fresh foods is also important, in particular so far as liver is concerned. Cats can become virtually addicted to liver and flatly refuse to eat anything else. However, liver in these quantities contains poisonous amounts of vitamin A, and serious spinal disease can result from this.

Many people believe that milk is essential to a cat's diet, but this is not the case. Some cats are not particularly fond of milk and simply leave it to turn sour, and even cats who do like milk should have a clean supply of water available in addition.

## CURIOSITY AND THE CAT

It is difficult to dissuade even the best-fed cat from investigating dustbins or piles of rubbish, especially when there is an intriguing smell. For this reason, ensure that all rubbish is put inside a securely closed bin, which is heavy enough to prevent the cat from toppling it over. It is also good practice to flatten all empty tins to prevent a cat's head from becoming stuck inside.

▲ *This foam bed, open with raised sides, has a luxurious lining of synthetic fur.*

■ **TABLE SCRAPS.** Many of your leftovers are tasty treats for your cat, such as bacon, fish or cheese scraps, etc. and one always feels less of a sense of waste when these items are consumed by a feline waste disposal unit. However it is quite unacceptable to attempt to feed a pet cat entirely on leftovers. Even if the quantity were sufficient, the balance of the diet would be completely inappropriate. Cats expected to exist on leftovers will be forced to supplement these either by hunting or by begging and stealing. This usually results in the cat becoming completely feral or simply moving in with another more generous family.

■ **WATER.** You will probably find that a cat fed a canned food diet drinks very little as he receives nearly all the moisture he needs from the food. However, various circumstances such as hot weather may dictate a need to drink more, and fresh clean water should always be available. Double food/water bowls are very useful for this purpose. Cats fed dry food, even in quite small amounts, will drink quite a lot of water because of the higher salt content in these foods. This is quite normal and is a deliberate modification of the foods to prevent the possible bladder problems mentioned earlier as being associated with these foods.

## BEDDING

■ **WHERE WILL YOUR CAT SLEEP?** A pet cat is rather like the 20-ton elephant in the old joke – he sleeps anywhere he likes! The best strategy to persuade him to sleep somewhere you approve of is therefore to make your chosen place into an attractive cat sleeping spot. Given an absolutely free choice, most cats will prefer your bed, preferably when are you are it. This is pleasant, cosy and companionable for you both, and apart from the risk of your bed becoming infested with fleas is really no more un-

desirable in health terms than any other contact you have with the cat. However, because of the problems of hairs, muddy paws, saliva slobber and threads snagged on sharp claws, many people would prefer to keep their cats off the bed. In this case it is best excluded from the bedroom entirely, by ensuring that the door is kept shut. You may find that even so he tends to cry and scratch at the bedroom door, and in this case you will have to restrict his movements so that he cannot approach the bedroom at night, for example by confining him to

## FELINE ACCESSORIES

**A** Enclosed foam cat bed
**B** Cardboard pet carrier
**C** Scratching post (most cats would prefer one a little taller than this)
**D** Plastic-covered wire mesh cat carrier
**E** Enclosed litter tray
**F** Open litter tray with litter
**G** Food or water bowl
**H** Toy catnip mouse
**I** Fine-tooth comb
**J** Soft brush
**K** Bell which can be attached to your cat's existing collar
**L** Collar with elastic insert and bell
**M** Small cannister which contains your cat's identification slip
**N** Toy ball with bell inside
**O** Catnip toy
**P** Toy ball with bell attached

another room. (This can be quite difficult to organize in some open-plan house designs.) If you choose to have his bedding in the kitchen, remember that you will have to contend with cat hairs on food preparation surfaces. Many cats are unhappy being confined in very small rooms. However, this is a reasonable option if you are worried about possible destructive behaviour at night.

Wherever you decide that he should sleep, you should try to make that place as attractive as possible in order to encourage use both at night and during the daytime. Cats like to sleep raised up above the floor, on a chair, shelf or worktop. They also like cosy enclosed spaces such as boxes or cupboards, which are free from air currents and give a feeling of security, so if you would prefer his bed on or near the floor, an enclosed bed is the answer. The one thing that cats love above all else is warmth, and if you really want to anchor your cat to a particular spot an electrically heated cat bed is almost certainly the answer. These are rated at about 20W and are quite inexpensive to leave switched on permanently.

■ **CAT BEDS.** If you visit a large pet shop, or even more so the stalls at a large cat show, you will find a bewildering variety of cat beds on sale. Cages are not to be considered here, being intended for breeders to keep queens with young litters safely confined and free from harassment, or to keep queens in heat separate from toms. The most popular beds are polystyrene (styrofoam) bead-filled bags, foam beds with raised sides (shaped like dog baskets) and enclosed foam beds with only a side opening for access. Bean bags are suitable for relaxed cats who like to sprawl around, while the foam beds give a greater feeling of security to cats who like to curl up. The enclosed beds are even more secure for nervous cats who like to hide in their own corner, and are really essential if you want your cat to sleep at floor level. Electrically heated pads may be used on their own but are even more attractive combined with a more comfortable bed. Although a bean bag or foam bed may not at first appear to insulate the cat from the heat, you will find that the heat does build up in the bed and when your cat lies on it it soon becomes very cosy. Of course it is not essential to purchase a custom-made cat bed, but these are usually made with ease of washing in mind and are nearly always much simpler to keep clean than cushions or blankets.

## HYGIENE

It is possible to train a cat to use the toilet, but it is a tedious and trying process, and it must be questioned whether the rather undignified result is really worth all the trouble, and if it is hygienic for you. The first question to consider is therefore whether you intend to give your cat an indoor litter tray or whether the garden will do.

■ **USING THE GARDEN.** The advantages of this arrangement are that you are spared the trouble of deciding where to put a litter tray, the expense of keeping it supplied with clean litter (which is not inconsiderable) and the work of cleaning and tidying the tray and disposing of the soiled litter. However it does mean that your cat must have reliable regular access outside to a suitable area, and that your plants are liable to be excavated from time to time. Most pet cats are extremely fastidious about burying their excreta, but even so a very small plot may become over-used, and neighbours may be less than enthusiastic if your cat uses part of a garden which is either not yours or part of a communal area.

One of the main problems with outside toileting is that, given the choice, most cats prefer the privacy (and

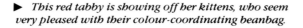

▶ *This red tabby is showing off her kittens, who seem very pleased with their colour-coordinating beanbag.*

CARING FOR YOUR CAT

the cleanliness) of their own litter tray. It is nearly always necessary when first acquiring your cat to keep him in-doors for a spell, when of course a litter tray must be provided. In any case most kittens from pet homes will have been trained to use a litter tray, and the problem may well lie in weaning them away from the thing. Simply removing it and shooing the cat outside when he seems to look for it (especially after meals) may work, but it may be necessary to move the tray itself out of doors, perhaps in gradual stages. If you do this, remember to site it in a covered location, or the litter will become saturated with rain, which is very unpleasant. A few cats resist this ploy entirely, and persist in performing indoors even if the tray is moved.

A healthy cat should not need to go outside much more often than every 12 hours or so, particularly if no dry food is being fed (which increases water consump-tion), and so a cat flap is not absolutely essential once you can rely on your cat, if you can be sure he is never left alone for too long. However, young kittens and elderly cats do have to go out more often and a cat flap then becomes preferable.

■ **LITTER TRAYS.** These are of course essential if you live in an upper flat or have no garden of your own, and in any situation they do save the garden from taking a beat-ing, allow you to leave your cat alone for longer periods without a cat flap, and are preferable for young kittens and older cats. The first question concerns siting of the tray. A kitchen is probably a bad place as food contamin-ation must be a risk. It is best to choose a spot away from constant traffic where the tray is not continually under-foot; which is easy to clean; and where a little bit of untidiness does not matter. A unused toilet or a back porch are good places, and in an apartment the bathroom itself may be best. Where space is really tight the tray may be best actually in the bath, which confines the litter and is easy to clean, though it does mean the tray must be tidied away before the bath can be used. For an indoor tray a commercial cat litter, though comparatively expen-sive, is virtually essential as garden earth or sand (even if you have access to an unlimited supply) does not have sufficient deodorizing capacity and both are very messy. You should experiment with several types of litter to find the one you and your cat prefer. Some cats take offence at

▲ *This cream Burmese seems a little unsure in the litter tray – perhaps because it is sited in too exposed a position.*

▲ *Cats frequently dislike being watched while using the garden – this mackerel tabby leaves no doubt as to what it is trying to tell you.*

▲ *Even small kittens should be properly supported when they are held, again with a hand under chest and hindquarters.*

the deodorizing additives in some types of litter and a more natural one may suit better in these cases.

Heavy, fuller's earth-based litters tend to clump when wet, and the easiest cleaning routine is to pour the loose, clean, dry litter into another tray and top this up if necessary, while the wet litter can then be scraped into newspaper and the first tray washed. Lightweight cat litters tend to disperse moisture and need only a quick shake to tidy the tray, until after a couple of days the whole lot must be cleaned out and replaced. Solid material should be regularly removed with a scoop and may be flushed down the toilet. Always be sure to give a generous filling of litter in a tray – miserly amounts in fact get wet and need replacing much more often. Be very conscious of hygiene when cleaning a tray – attend to it frequently, wear disposable rubber gloves, wash these after cleaning the tray, and dispose of all soiled material by wrapping in several layers of newspaper then sealing in a plastic bag. Few things are nastier than loose cat litter in a dustbin or wastepaper basket! Litter trays should be washed separately from any other household items and disinfected regularly. Pregnant women must *never* handle a litter tray because of the risks of toxoplasmosis (Chapter 6).

Several variations on the basic litter tray are available. Larger cats will appreciate a larger tray, and the trays which come with a high clip-on lid with only a side access hole are not just intended to spare the blushes of the modest kitty, but do aid tidiness by preventing litter from being kicked all over the room. In any case, a few sheets of newspaper under the tray will help confine the mess and return it where it belongs. More complicated patent contraptions such as double-decker trays with reusable granules tend to be less popular, but you may fine one that is just what you need.

## HANDLING YOUR CAT

While it is true that a mother cat picks up her kittens by the scruff of the neck, this is only suitable for very young light kittens and is a most unkind way of handling an adult cat. Adults should be picked up and held by supporting them at two points – under the chest just behind the elbows, and under the hindquarters. Avoid picking a cat up by the abdomen as this is also most uncomfortable.

Firmer handling will be needed if you want to do anything the cat may not like much, such as give him a tablet or clean his ears. This is easy if someone else can hold him, but if you are singlehanded a good tip is to kneel down, sitting on your heels with your knees apart on the floor. The cat can be restrained by backing him against your body (your heels prevent him escaping backwards), which leaves your hands free to manipulate his head. The easiest way to open a cat's mouth is to place one hand over the top of his head with finger and thumb

grasping under each cheek bone, and tilt his head upwards. Use the forefinger of the other hand to open his mouth and insert a tablet right at the back, pushing it over the back of the tongue.

To clean the ears, take hold of the ear flap firmly with one hand and pull it upwards, grasping the cat's head at the same time, and clean gently with a damp cotton bud (cotton swab). So long as you do not lose sight of the cotton tip there is no danger of going too far into the ear. This method will not prevent a determined cat from scratching but it will give you the best chance.

Most cats thoroughly dislike flea sprays and hide whenever one is produced. Once you have lured your cat from under the sofa the best and quickest way to apply the spray is to grasp him by the scruff of the neck and sit him up on his hindquarters with your left hand, while the right hand wields the can. This is not especially comfortable, but it will hold the cat helpless for the necessary five seconds. However, you should not attempt to lift it right off the ground in this way.

For other necessary unpleasantness such as grooming a matted coat, giving a bath or cleaning a wound, the firm grasp on the scruff of the neck is again the most effective restraint. The aim in this case should be to hold the cat still by pressing *down* with the hand holding the scruff. Be as gentle as you can, but above all be firm and do not give up, as it is no kindness to leave soiling or wounds unattended to just because your cat resents being handled. If he is really violent and lashes out with teeth and claws, a pair of stout leather gloves is the answer. Motorcycling gloves with gauntlets usually provide effective protection.

## COLLARS AND HARNESSES

Few people bother to train their cats to walk on a leash, but it is very important to make sure that all kittens become accustomed to a collar from as early an age as possible. This is because of the necessity for *identifying* a cat. A collar shows he is not a stray, which may on the one hand save him from being persecuted and on the other prevent him from being adopted by another family. Several very unpleasant court cases could have been avoided if the object of the dispute had been wearing a collar. In addition, a name tag will allow you to be contacted if your cat is discovered lost or injured, or in the worst case may save you from never finding out what has become of him if he is found killed. It is sad to have to bury what is obviously a pet cat when there is no way to contact the owners. Your cat may not care for a collar at first, but you should insist until he gets used to it. Medallion name tags can be awkward if you have a long address to squeeze on, but they can be read without removing them, while message-capsule type tags must be unscrewed, and if your cat strolls off at this point you may never get the

▲ *A harness and lead allow a cat to be exercised in a strange garden with little risk of escape.*

▶ *Kittens usually catch on to the function of a cat flap very quickly. This one has been fitted in an outside wall, above the damp course, rather than in a door.*

cylinder part back! Many people believe that their cat looks better without a collar, and this may be so, but the risk is not really worth it. You will find that smooth collars (rather than felt) catch the hair less, especially in long-hairs, and you can experiment with different colours to find the most attractive match. Metallic-effect collars can look very striking and come in several colours. Reflective strips on collars can be a useful safety feature, while some of the newer types of flea collar are quite presentable. Whichever you choose, make sure there is an elasticated strip incorporated and that it is not so tight that the cat cannot wriggle his head free from a snagged collar fairly easily. If you do this the chances of him becoming caught up on a branch are extremely small.

A cat should never, ever, be tied up – if you want to restrain him completely, use a basket. However, it is often useful to be able to attach your cat to yourself, for example to get him used to a strange garden or to allow some relief during a long journey if no litter tray is available. For this purpose a body harness is necessary as a leash should not be attached to a cat's collar. A harness should be fitted as tightly as possible without causing discomfort,

but even so he will probably be able to wriggle out if he can pull against the leash and so the aim should be to follow the cat's movements and gently restrain him rather than to provoke a full-scale battle. Begin by fitting the harness alone indoors for short periods, then attach the leash – a long string is better than a regular leash but may tangle, and a retractable 'flexi-leash' as sold for small dogs is best. At first simply follow the cat around, avoiding entanglements, then accustom him to gentle restraint on the harness. The object is to prevent him from leaping away for just long enough for you to pick him up, not use force. Then the exercise may be extended out of doors. Most people are content with this level of restraint on a cat, but it is possible to continue the training towards actual walking on a leash, although it is virtually impossible to induce a cat to walk to heel.

## YOUR CAT AND YOUR LIFESTYLE

Cats are much less demanding than dogs, and much more tolerant of a busy lifestyle. In fact they can be so flexible that the only people who should not consider

having a cat are probably those who are frequently absent from home for periods of more than 10–12 hours.

Some people believe that cats should never be allowed out to face the dangers of the streets or fields, while other claim that it is unkind to confine a cat. As with most questions, this depends on the circumstances. Kittens born indoors and kept in fairly spacious rooms with plenty of toys and scope for exercise will probably never miss what they have never known; this may be the only option in very busy urban areas. Conversely, cats in quiet residential districts or country areas will enjoy roaming and embarking on the occasional hunting trip. A cat flap in an outside door will provide the maximum freedom, but unless you choose one with an electronic key for the cat's collar, any other cat will also be able to get in. Most cats are fairly content to have access in or out only when a human doorkeeper is in attendance. So far as putting the cat out at night is concerned, you should realize that the majority of accidents involving cats occur at night and the majority of missing cats are reported as failing to return in the morning. It is therefore desirable to encourage your cat to come indoors before you retire to bed, and, depending on the degree of danger in your area, it may be best to lock any cat flap until morning. Even dedicated hunters usually prefer to return home to sleep later at night, and so if you cannot bring your cat in before you go to bed then an open cat flap or a safe, secure, comfortable bed in a garage or outhouse will be needed.

While it is certainly unfair to keep a cat if you are away from home for 18-hour periods several times a week, it is certainly possible to leave a cat occasionally for this length of time, for example if you wish to go directly from work to an evening out. It is only necessary to ensure that the litter tray (if used – if not a cat flap is essential) is clean and that sufficient food is left out. Most cats will continue their regular eating habits of frequent small meals, but special timer-operated cat dishes are available with lids which open at pre-set times. These will discourage gobblers from stuffing themselves with the lot in one sitting and protect against contamination of the food. When you return you may find your cat following you around and mewing, even though he has food and does not need to go out. What he wants is a cuddle as compensation for being abandoned.

If you live alone and plan to be away for more than about 18 hours, you should not leave your cat to fend for himself even if he is very independent; make appropriate special arrangements, as if for a holiday (see Chapter 4).

▶ *A shorthair like this Russian Blue will need only a soft brush for grooming, rather than a comb. The use of newspaper not only protects the carpet but allows any evidence of flea dirt falling from the coat to be easily appreciated.*

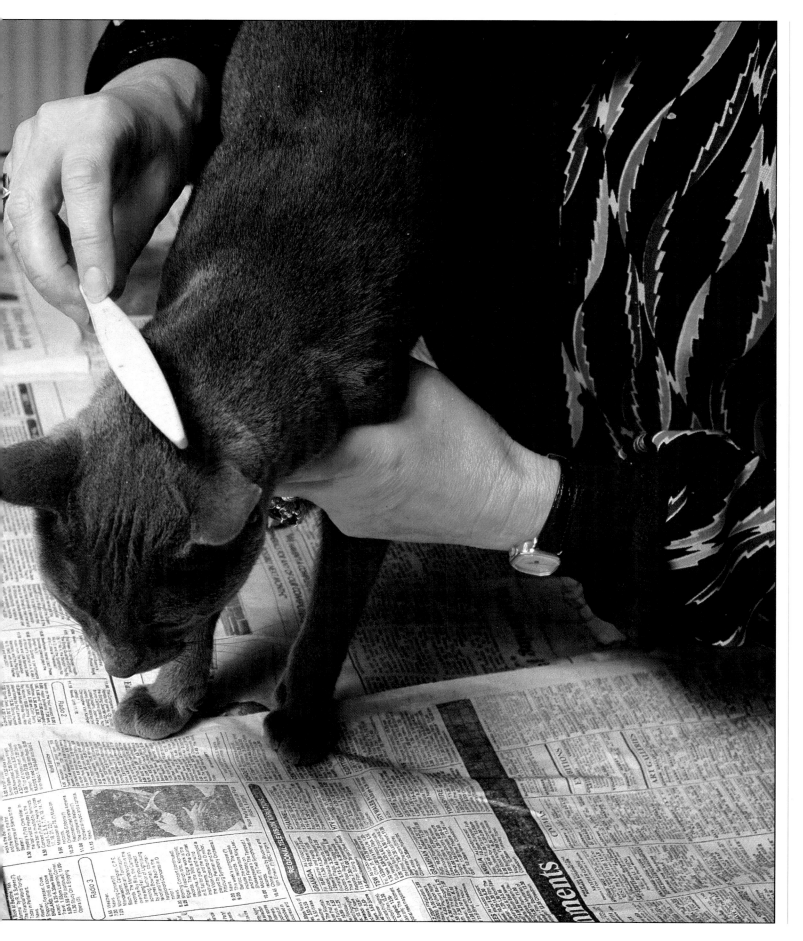

CARING FOR YOUR CAT

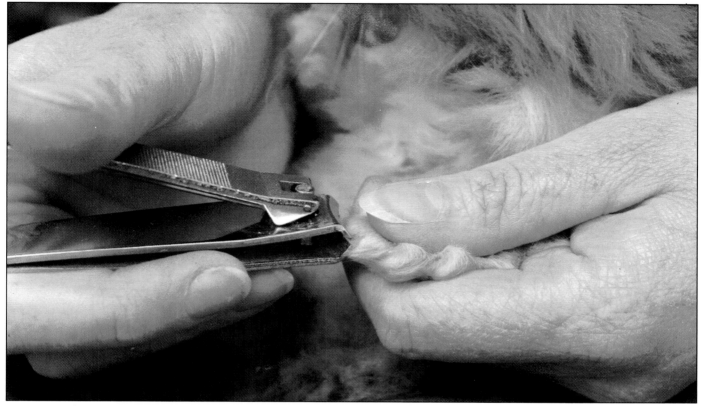

▲ *Clipping of the tips of the claws is not essential, but it is a requirement of some cat show organising bodies.*

◀ *Thorough cleaning of the ears is part of show grooming, but otherwise this procedure would only be necessary to deal with the aftermath of an ear mite infestation.*

## GROOMING

■ **GENERAL GROOMING AND THE SHORTHAIR.** Shorthairs require minimal grooming to keep their coats in order, but it is wise to establish a weekly routine in order to become familiar with your cat's body so that any abnormalities can be recognized as such and any developing problems caught at an early stage. Kittens should be accustomed to gentle brushing from a fairly young age, but shorthairs are usually quite tolerant of a soft brush even when introduced to this as adults. Place the cat on a clean white surface for brushing and examine the brushings for flea dirt – tiny black 'corkscrews' that smear rusty red when wet – or fleas, and be sure to remove any mud or small tangles. Part the hair to check the roots for flea dirt. Run your hands over his body to check for scars or wounds. Check eyes and nose for discharges: you should not need to wipe anything away. Check his ears for mites. Ears should be absolutely clean or only show the tiniest amount of wax, and any reddish gritty encrustations certainly require veterinary attention. Check his teeth to assess the current state of any tartar or gingivitis, especially the outside faces of the top molars which can be inspected by pulling the top lip upwards and backwards. Check his claws for splits or ragged edges, and check under his tail

for sore spots or tapeworm segments. These appear either fresh as little white motile packets emerging from the anus or dried up like grains of rice sticking to the hair. This routine need take only a few minutes and is a valuable part of preventive health care. If flea control sprays are used then a five-second spray should be applied after grooming every two weeks.

■ **THE LONGHAIR.** All of the above applies also to the longhair, but the necessity for attending to the long coat makes for a more lengthy routine and requires a comb to be employed. Semi-longhair cats may need a thorough grooming perhaps only once a week, but true longhairs *must* be combed *daily* to avoid matting. Ensure the whole cat is combed, especially under the elbows, between the hind legs, and the sides of the tail. Many longhairs resent the comb, especially if there are tangles and mats to tease out, and it is therefore vitally important to accustom a longhair kitten to gentle combing from an early age. Otherwise the matting problem will become intractable, and the harder you try the more the cat will be hurt and the worse his behaviour will become. At this stage the only solution is a trip to the vet for a 'de-mat' under general anaesthetic, which will solve the problem for the time being, but it is necessary then to make a determined effort to establish the daily combing routine if the 'de-

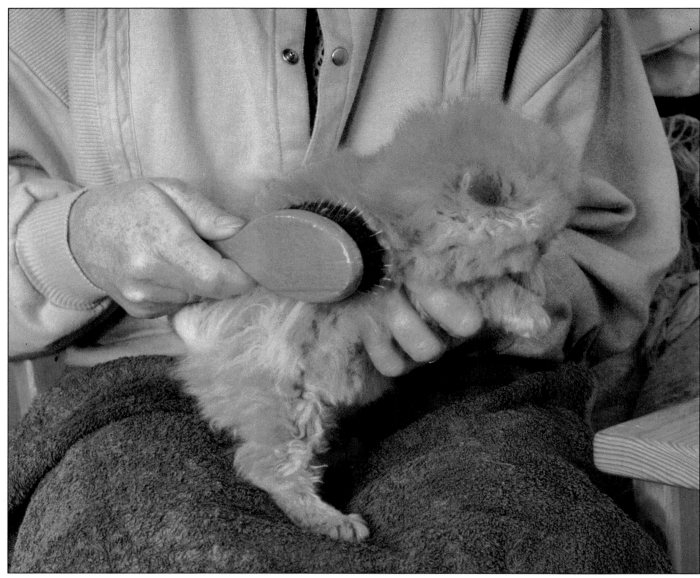

▲ *If you start thorough grooming early, most cats grow to love it.*
▶ *Cats' eyes need regular and careful wiping, though face the cat when you are doing this.*

mat' is not to become a regular six-monthly occurrence. In a longhair the checks for fleas and ear mites should be particularly thorough as the long coat can conceal all sorts of nasties.

■ **SHOW GROOMING.** This is a very specialized subject, and if you intend to show a particular breed you should consult experienced exhibitors of that breed for the expert tips. Many cats will require bathing, particularly light-coloured cats, those with extensive white areas and most longhairs, although smaller white patches may be washed individually. Bathing will remove the oil and gloss from the coat so ideally should be done at least a week before the show, but then you have the problem of keeping the cat clean! If powder grooming preparations are used most show rules require that no trace be left on the coat. In general one would begin with a thorough

regular grooming, then wipe clean the paws and claws and under the tail. Some show regulations require the tip to be clipped from the end of each claw. The ears should be carefully cleaned of all trace of wax with a damp cotton bud (cotton swab), and the eyes and nose carefully wiped with a damp cloth. Take care to avoid getting the cloth *into* the eye as the irritation may resemble an eye infection which would result in your cat being rejected at the veterinary inspection. Finally, give the coat a polish with a piece of velvet. Most of this can be done the evening before the show, but give a final once-over before penning and be sure to wipe the last traces of breakfast away!

■ **BATHING.** This may be necessary as routine in order to show certain breeds, but more usually it is an emergency situation where a cat has become heavily soiled or a heavy

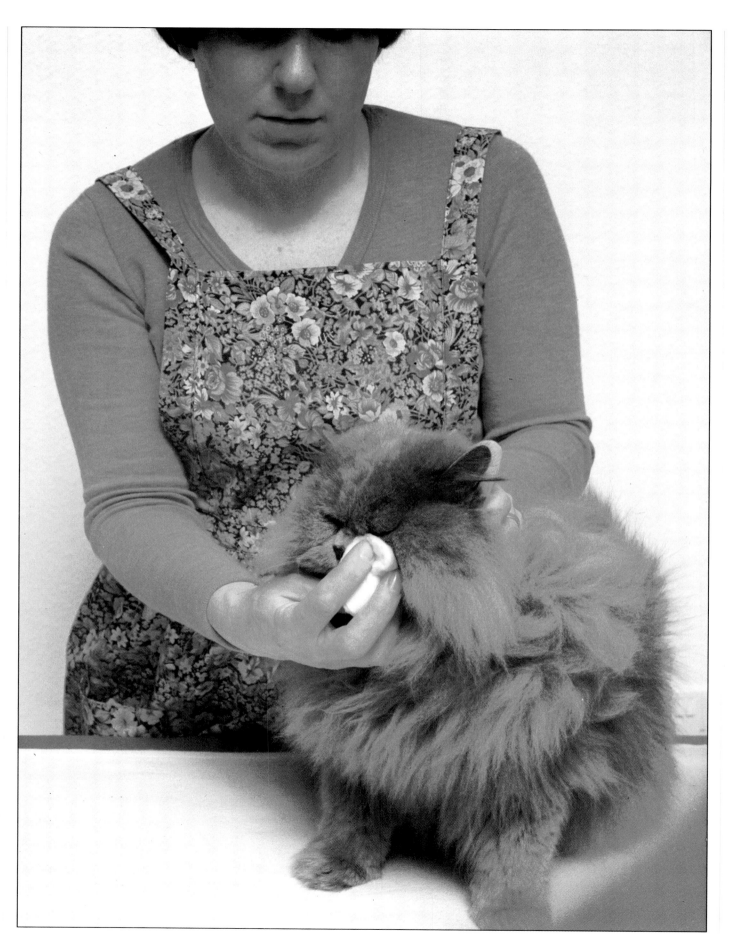

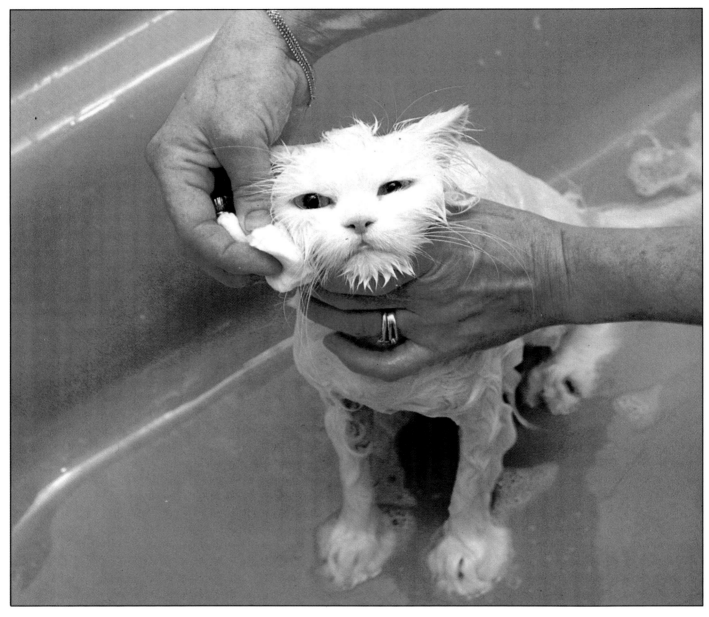

▲ *This white Persian is clearly well accustomed to the bath which is essential to keep such a coat in show condition – very few ordinary cats would accept this treatment so calmly.*

flea infestation has left thick deposits of flea dirt. If mud, dirt or flea dirt is the problem, thorough bathing will suffice, but if oil, paint or chemical spillage is suspected you should obtain your vet's advice on how best to tackle these substances. A bathroom or utility room is a more satisfactory place than a kitchen to bathe an animal, and a spray attachment is very useful. Before beginning, plug the cat's ears with a small wad of cotton wool. Make sure the water, whether in a spray or basin, is lukewarm. Provide a non-slip surface for the cat to stand on, such as a rubber mat, either on the bottom of the sink with the basin of water on the side or in the bath, and gently wet the coat all over using the spray or a plastic cup.

It has been suggested that the easiest way is for you to join the cat and the bowl of water in the bath, preferably wearing a bathing costume! Be prepared to be firm (though gentle) in your restraint and try to avoid complicated ju-jitsu manoeuvres. A harness may be a useful aid, but a firm grasp of the scruff of the neck is usually the most effective restraint. Animal shampoos are available but human ones (preferably baby shampoo) will do if you do not require an anti-parasitic preparation. Use just enough to work up a light lather, and be very careful to avoid the eyes, ears, nose and mouth. If the shampoo must be left on for some time (as in some anti-parasitic shampoos) keep the cat warm and prevent him from licking the coat. If soiling is heavy, two shampoo applications may be needed, rinsing between. Your cat may allow you to rinse him by immersion in a bowl or sink, otherwise use the spray or cup with plenty of clean water until

▲ *It is important to ensure that the shampoo is thoroughly rinsed off, especially when it contains an insecticide – otherwise the cat may ingest it when grooming himself.*

the hair 'squeaks'. Then squeeze and towel as much water from the coat as possible and keep the cat in a very warm place, combing the coat occasionally, until he is quite dry. This may be speeded up if your cat will tolerate the use of a hair dryer, set on 'low.' Remember also to remove the cotton wool from his ears. Then find some antiseptic and bandages for your scratches and be sure to explain the situation to any acquaintances who might otherwise draw the understandable conclusion that you have been trying to slit your wrists with a razor.

## TRAVELLING WITH YOUR CAT

The first essential for travelling with your cat is a cat basket, as it is very risky even to walk a short distance to the vet with the cat in your arms. Cat baskets come in many materials and shapes. Wicker is well ventilated, quite light, and feels secure for the cat. Solid plastic is cosy but needs ventilation holes, and clear plastic must be very disconcerting for a nervous occupant. Plastic-covered wire mesh is favoured by vets as it is secure, the occupant can be seen, and it is easily cleaned, but again it is draughty and may not feel very secure unless a cover is fitted. Top-opening lids are much more escape-proof than side doors in most cases, but the resulting square basket can be very awkward to carry. Cardboard pet carrier cartons are all very well in an emergency but are most certainly not escape-proof (they can be shredded from around the air holes) and do not last long.

When purchasing a carrier, make sure it will be large

▲ *This fully grown Persian is very relaxed, even during the ticklish parts – this is essential to allow the thorough combing needed to prevent such a luxurious coat from matting.*

◄ *Longhaired kittens, especially Persian types, should be accustomed to the grooming routine from a very early age.*

enough for your cat as an adult, but also that it is not too difficult to carry. Two cats may share a carrier, but again consider what size and weight you can manage. You may find that shutting him in the carrier inside the house is counter-productive, as he cannot see why he is confined and may attempt to escape, and you may prefer to carry the cat on a short walk around the garden or have him sit inside the carrier in the car for a short time to let him get used to it. Keep a close eye out for cunning escape strategies, as you may have to add extra ties or straps to thwart the budding Houdini. So long as the basket is comfortable (bed it with a small blanket or an old pullover, not a cushion as that will be too bulky) any cat will probably settle down quite happily, and may even go into the basket of his own accord for security in strange surroundings.

Long journeys pose particular problems, whether by car or public transport. You may enquire about sedatives from your vet, but in general these are not recommended for cats as in some cases they have the opposite effect and the cat goes quite berserk. Try to avoid long journeys until you feel you can trust your cat to settle in the basket for long periods, especially where public transport is involved. When travelling by car, do not take the cat out of the basket as a loose cat is extremely dangerous in a moving vehicle.

Provided he settles well, the call of nature is the main problem; he is unlikely to need or want any food. This is one situation where a harness and flexible leash can be very useful, allowing you to take him to any convenient piece of waste ground at a railway station or

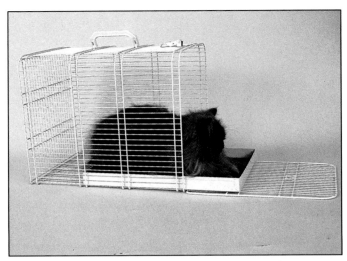

▲ *This carrying case incorporates an ingenious method of extracting a reticent cat – and the base could even double up as a litter tray if necessary.*

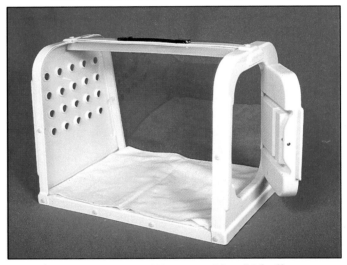

▲ *This carrier has solid perspex sides which allows a curious cat to watch what is going on around him.*

motorway service area. You should also offer water at such stops. In summer the main danger to be aware of is over-heating leading to heat stroke. Open-mouthed panting is the main sign of distress to watch for. If you see this, take him to a cool shady place immediately until behaviour is normal, offer him water, and be particularly careful when you set off again. If the cat seems seriously disturbed or collapsed, immerse as much of its body as possible in cold water and seek veterinary attention immediately. In this event it is extremely unwise to attempt to resume the journey before the following day.

Taking or sending a cat on an air journey poses particular problems which should be discussed with your travel agent and vet. Short flights may present little difficulty, but on long flights where a cat may be confined to a small cage in a cargo hold, unattended and with limited food and water, it may be wiser to consider finding another method of transporting the cat. For major events such as emigration there are firms which specialize in pet transport, and your vet may be able to put you in touch with one of these.

## INSURANCE

Your cat may not have cost as much as your car, but if he breaks a leg or goes down with a serious illness the resulting bill can make the damage for a moderate car crash look like small change. Veterinary surgeons (veterinarians) are in the main caring, compassionage people, but they are also running a private business with a mortgage to pay, and often several children and assorted pets of their own to feed. They are therefore not in a position to offer charity treatment no matter how touching your pet's plight may be. There are animal charities and welfare societies to assist people genuinely unable to afford veterinary fees, but for most people on average incomes a pet health insurance policy is the answer. Your vet may be able to recommend one or two suitable policies for you to choose from, and in any case you should enquire whether in his or her experience your chosen company is reasonable to deal with when making a claim. Before deciding, read the small print carefully and pay particular attention to all the exclusion clauses – this can prevent a nasty surprise.

It is always best to begin insurance when your pet is as young as possible. The routine veterinary care of young animals, such as worming, vaccination and neutering, is of course not covered, but many companies refuse to issue new policies on older animals and any which do issue them load the premiums very heavily. Ensure that you comply with all requirements such as keeping vaccinations up to date, and consider carefully the question of excess payments versus upper limits. It is much better to commit yourself to an excess payment of a modest sum so long as there is no ceiling, or a very high one, on the claims, rather than to accept a low ceiling which may result in a large bill in the case of a serious illness. Be particularly aware that a single claim is generally for the whole of a specific illness or course of treatment rather than for each individual visit or consultation. Before authorizing an expensive course of treatment it is always wise to check that the insurance company do consider themselves liable – otherwise you will be required to pay the bill.

In most countries you are not legally liable for any damage or accident your cat may be responsible for, and so you will not be able to insure against this. It is also unlikely that you will be able to insure your house contents against damage by the cat, but some 'accidental risks' policies may cover this and it is worth checking household policy schedules to ascertain which pet-associated risks are covered.

## CHAPTER THREE

# Cat Behaviour

▲ *Cats at play are most engaging to watch.*

## SLEEPING

It may seem peculiar to begin a discussion of cat behaviour with a section on sleeping, but this probably occupies most cats for most of the day. It is not really true that cats are nocturnal animals in the strict sense of the word. Like all carnivores, for whom food gathering occupies only a relatively small amount of their time, a great deal of the remaining time, while the prey is being digested, is spent in sleep. This applies both during the day and during the night. In addition, the best time for hunting small rodents and birds, the cat's natural prey, is late evening and sometimes early morning. This means that most cats tend to prick up their ears and twitch their whiskers around bedtime on fine nights, and if they embark on a hunting trip then, they may perforce stay out all night if they cannot gain access to the house when they return. However, cats with free access through a cat flap frequently return to bed quite early in the night, perhaps making a sortie again at dawn. These cats usually seem to fare quite well, and it appears to be those who are forced to roam the streets all night because of a mistaken belief on the part of their owners that it is correct to put the cat out at night who are most often involved in accidents. Just because your cat sleeps ten hours a day does not mean he will not be quite happy to sleep ten hours a night as well!

## GROOMING AND CLAW SHARPENING

It is highly entertaining to watch a cat grooming himself, as the complicated attitudes eclipse those of the most talented circus contortionist. The cat's tongue is very well adapted for grooming, being covered with numerous hard, sharp, backward-curving spines like the teeth of a comb. (These are also used to lap water when drinking and in tearing and ingesting the prey.) The tongue has the facility for reaching almost every hair, and only the face and ears require washing 'second-hand' using the inner surfaces of the forepaws, well licked. As well as keeping the coat clean, this grooming behaviour provides one form of 'displacement activity,' when a cat is unsure of what to do next. Any cat confronted with a dilemma or an uncertain situation will give his shoulder a few quick licks, and in the home environment a cat who seems to be embarrassed will do the same. In one sense it gives the dilemma a chance to resolve itself, and in another it seems to give the message 'well, I am doing something else anyway' to the casual observer.

▲ *Three Siamese cuddle up for a cat-nap beside the sofa.*

CAT BEHAVIOUR

▲ *The feline body is so flexible that even the underside of the tail can be washed with ease.*

◄ *Sometimes cats groom if they are embarrassed: it is then called displacement activity.*

One unfortunate side-effect of grooming behaviour is that the backward-curving spines cause a lot of hair to be swallowed. It is natural for this to pass straight through or be vomited up as a hair ball (usually on the best carpet), but sometimes a persistent hair ball in the stomach or intestines requires treatment. This problem is much more severe with longhairs, which is another reason for being rigid to a frequent grooming schedule. If you observe a real Persian-type longhair you will see that the tongue does not act nearly so efficiently on the long coat, which is why these coats mat so easily.

Unlike dogs, cats have retractable claws which do not wear down when walking. Instead, cats pull the old husk of nail from their claws by raking them down some convenient piece of wood, to expose a new sharp claw underneath. To do this they stretch high up a fence post

or tree, dig in their claws, and pull. This is also to some extent a territory-marking activity, and it may be that the height of the marks is intended to warn of the size of the cat making them. Cats who confine this activity to the garden, or perhaps make do indoors with horizontal claw sharpening on a carpet (which seems to do no harm) are all very well, but when the sofa and the wallpaper become the scratching posts it is time to do something. As always with cats, a simple *no* usually has very little effect, and much better results will be obtained by providing a permitted scratching post, usually a carpet-covered post on a solid stand, and indicate that he should use this instead. Discouraging tactics such as hanging tinfoil over the threatened items are usually very effective, but a really intractable vandal may have to be permanently excluded from the best rooms in the house. Some vets are prepared

CAT BEHAVIOUR

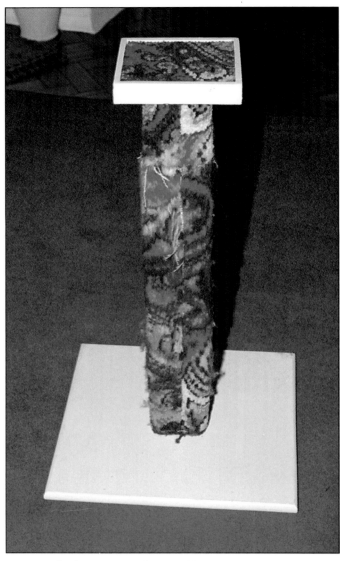

▲ *A custom-made scratching post will deflect attention from the furniture – but it must be very solid, and with a base large enough to prevent it from toppling.*

▶ *Claw sharpening out of doors. It is wise to protect young trees from cats, as the bark may be stripped off.*

to consider removing the claws on a cat's forepaws surgically if they are convinced that it is the only alternative to enthanasia, but most feel that the mutilation is quite un-ethical as a declawed cat is almost defenceless, cannot climb at all, and is very insecure jumping any more than very short distances.

## TERRITORIAL BEHAVIOUR

Cats are in general very territorial animals, and even pet cats who are more concerned with their people than their actual territory exhibit clear territory marking behaviour – often in fact marking their owners. The strongest, and by far the most unpleasant, territory marker is the urine spray, usually only exhibited by males which

CAT BEHAVIOUR

▲ *Having killed a rabbit, this tortoiseshell may be bringing it home as a present for her unsuspecting owner.*
◄ *A tom cat marks his territory by urine spraying. Even outdoors like this the smell can be very objectionable.*

have not been neutered. In these cats the urine has a truly appalling stench, and is sprayed on territory objects in a movement quite unlike normal urination, with the tom backing up against the object and spraying a fine mist with tail raised and hind paws paddling. Neutered males and females who acquire this behaviour pattern do not of course smell quite so objectionable, but are a major nuisance nonetheless as it can be difficult to break the habit. Hormone treatment may sometimes help.

The more universal, and fortunately less repulsive, territory marking method is carried out by rubbing the side of the face against the corners of doors, furniture, etc. There are scent glands on the sides of a cat's face which transfer his particular odour to the mark, and you can often see a cat sniffing at marks made by other cats before adding a layer of his own. It may be wise to protect any vulnerable corners of wallpaper in the house with clear sticky-backed plastic before any real damage is

done, but you will find yourself going round cleaning the little brown stains away on a fairly regular basis. Cats also extend this activity to rubbing the sides of their bodies against such places, and when your cat rubs itself against your legs he is in a way saying 'you are mine'!

## HUNTING AND PLAY

Cats have a very highly-developed hunting instinct, which thousands of generations of domestication do not seem to have dulled. This instinct is so strong that even cats who dine regularly on the most expensive canned food will demonstrate enthusiastic hunting behaviour. This is part of what it is to be a cat, and discouraging tactics, even punishment, will have little effect. You may circumvent your cat's wiles to some extent by arranging a high bird-table out of his reach and keeping your hamster in a very solid cage, but you should realize that a certain amount of

CAT BEHAVIOUR

## TERRITORY MARKING

A cat rubs first his face, then the whole length of his body to the tail, to transfer his scent to the fence, thus marking it as his territory.

predatory behaviour must be accepted in the majority of cats. Of course this behaviour has its positive aspects, in that a good mouser can be a great advantage in older properties and around stables and farmyards. It is certainly not necessary to keep a cat short of food to encourage hunting, and in fact well-fed cats are often more efficient as they are less anxious and in better general health.

Cats learn to hunt by observing their mothers, who display exaggerated hunting behaviour in front of their litters. At first the hunting movements are random and disconnected, then they are gradually put together as play routines and mock battles. Pet cats, who have their needs provided for by a 'parent' figure throughout their lives, do in some ways continue to display kittenish behaviour as adults, and the most striking example of this is in play. Even a dignified older cat will be seen on occasion stalking a stuffed mouse or killing a ping-pong ball, and companion cats will often indulge in the mock battles and chasing games typical of growing kittens. Unlike most dogs, adult cats will often play quite happily when alone and it is wise to give your cat some toys of his own and to leave them accessible, otherwise you may not approve of the objects he decides to involve in his games.

It is this association of play with hunting which perhaps distresses pet-owners most, as cats seem to be taking a sadistic delight in tormenting their prey rather than going for a quick kill. However, the reason for this is that cats depend almost entirely on a very precise and quick bite to make the actual kill, and, due to their short faces and fairly small teeth, they are actually very vulnerable to facial injury at that moment, especially from rodents. The 'play' routine, with its periods of waiting and darting in and out, has evolved to give cats the best chance of a good opportunity for biting at the safest possible moment, and has nothing to do with sadistic pleasure. This is simply the way cats are, and you might as well punish them for purring as for 'tormenting' an injured bird.

### PURRING AND VOCALISATION

Cats have a fairly wide vocabulary of sounds, and after a suitable period of training by the cat, most owners are able to understand what their pet wants just as clearly as parents know why their baby is crying. Different miaows can be distinguished which mean 'I want in,' 'I want out,' 'I want feeding,' 'I am pleased to see you,' 'Do you really expect me to eat this stuff?' and so on. Many cats actually initiate conversations with their owners, miaowing when spoken to, and after ten minutes or so of this type of exchange the owner is usually left feeling that something of major significance has just been discussed, but only the cat knows what it is!

Louder sounds are used during sexual encounters, by both males and females, and anyone who has ever tried

▲ *This hiss is very definitely a warning, clearly saying 'stay clear of my territory!'*

to get to sleep near a cats' meeting place on a fine night will know exactly what this caterwauling sounds like. Loud noises also accompany aggressive behaviour, in conjunction with hissing and growling, but the most efficient hunters stalk and capture their prey in silence.

Purring is a peculiar sound unique to felidae, and, oddly enough, no one is entirely sure just how cats actually make the sound. It is generally believed to be a sign of pleasure and relaxation, and indeed this is usually the case. However, the purr is also to some extent a sign of absence of hostile intent, or even of submission. So, a dominant cat may purr to reassure an inferior that his intentions are friendly, and an inferior may purr to indicate that he does not wish to challenge. An injured cat

CAT BEHAVIOUR

▲ *Even at this young age the play movements of these cream Persian kittens reveal their predatory nature.*

◄ *Two cats playing tug-o'-war. The one lying on the carpet clearly shows the characteristic parallel stripes of the mackerel tabby.*

often purrs on the vet's examination table. It may indeed indicate that he knows he is being helped, but there is certainly an element in this situation of the terrified cat who is saying simply 'Please don't hurt me!'

## SOCIAL BEHAVIOUR

Cats live in close-knit family groups only up to the age of weaning, and in rather looser association with the mother and littermates until puberty. Thereafter the adult cat without kittens does conform to a certain extent to the image of the solitary 'cat who walks by himself'. The main exception to this is in households where a number of cats are kept together, where an extended litter-companionship situation is in force. This is why this situation is most easily set up by adopting two or more kittens from one litter, and when a new cat or kitten is introduced to a household with an established cat there is usually a period

## FELINE AFFECTION

▲ *A cat rubbing up against your legs is a sign of affection – but it also serves as territory marking.*

▲ *Feline sexual behaviour is violent; when an affectionate cat suddenly turns nasty be has forgotten be is not playing with another cat.*

of jealousy and sulks to go through before a littermate by adoption relationship grows. However, although cats will prefer to live and hunt alone, they are seldom happy if kept in complete isolation from others of their species. House cats who have access outside will indeed avoid other cats while hunting, but at other times neighbouring cats, including neutered ones, will occasionally seek out company, and sometimes sit around in groups or indulge in mutual grooming. This behaviour is probably quite important to the cat, and in situations where a cat is to be kept permanently indoors with no opportunity for social interaction then serious consideration should be given to acquiring a pair of littermates rather than a single kitten.

Cats do not display the same rigid hierarchical structure as do groups of dogs. In a cattery there may be one 'boss cat' who has first choice of food and sleeping place, and perhaps one or two timid individuals who tend to be pushed around, but in between there is little structure. This may be the reason why so many cat encounters end up as fights, as there is no predetermined agreement as to which one will back off from the situation.

### TRAINING

Most cat-owners will agree that, even when they begin with the intention of training their cat, the eventual result is that the shoe goes on the other foot and the cat ends up with a well-trained human at his beck and call. This is partly accomplished by the cat playing on the parental instincts of the owner, as many cat sounds do bear a strong resemblance to babies' cries, and is partly a natural 'anything-for-a-quiet-life' reaction by the owners on finding themselves fighting a losing battle. Cats do not possess the doggy facility of gaining pleasure from doing things just because it makes their owners happy, and simply do not accept 'because I say so' as a valid reason for doing anything at all. This does not mean that your cat loves you any less than your dog does, but it is in his nature rather to present you with a half-chewed mouse as a sign of affection (which is, after all, entirely his own idea), than to jump through hoops with a fatuous grin.

For most people, therefore, training a cat is limited to such necessities as using a litter tray, sleeping in an approved spot, using a scratching post rather than the Chippendale and occasionally coming when called. As discussed earlier, the tactics to be adopted are those of persuasion rather than coercion, whereby the approved sleeping place is made more comfortable and attractive than any alternative, and the scratching post made more inviting than the sofa. 'Training' therefore becomes less a case of 'No, don't do that!' and more 'Why don't you try this instead?' And most people will agree that the most effective cat callers known are the sounds of a can-opener or a box of dry cat food being shaken.

▲ *Threatened out of doors, this longhair arches his back and fluffs out his fur to make himself appear much larger and more formidable than he really is.*

CAT BEHAVIOUR

## A MOCK BATTLE

Although it may look serious, these two cats are more than half playing. However, it is quite likely that bites and scratches will occur when a game becomes as violent as this.

It is certainly possible to take cat training further than this, as cats are not stupid, and mentally just as capable as dogs of learning complex routines. Many hundreds of cats are successfully trained for advertising, film and television work each year. However, lacking the pleasure-through-pleasing reaction of the dog, cats require much more patience and tactful handling to persuade them to respond to commands. This sort of work therefore involves a fair amount of skill and judgement if the cat is not to become frustrated and resentful.

Punishing a cat is something to be considered only in truly serious circumstances, and even then the danger of the punishment being counter-productive is always present. As a cat will not do something just because it pleases you, he will not *refrain* from doing something in order to please you. He is therefore likely to associate any punishment with you yourself rather than with his behaviour, resentment will develop, and he may actually continue the forbidden actions just in order to spite you. It is usually much more productive simply to make it impossible for the cat to do what you do not want him to do, or arrange some sort of aversion booby trap to dissuade him, such as hanging tinfoil or balloons around an object which you would prefer him not to claw.

### BEHAVIOURAL PROBLEMS

Behavioural problems in cats almost always take the form of inappropriate displays of normal behavioural patterns such as territory marking, claw sharpening and aggressive interaction, and an understanding of the type of behaviour pattern involved and the normal circumstances of its expression is important when attempting to deal with this. Relatively minor problems can usually be successfully tackled by providing the cat with an acceptable means of expressing that behaviour as a substitute for the unacceptable, as in providing a scratching post to spare the sofa.

A serious behavioural problem is nearly always the response of a cat to a situation which he simply cannot come to terms with. For example, an older cat may begin spray-marking in the house because he feels his territory is being threatened by an intruder, or a cat may persistently shred the furniture because he cannot cope with being confined permanently indoors. Obviously the best remedy is to remove the cause, once identified, but clearly in many situations this is simply not possible. However, the application of a little cat psychology can often resolve or alleviate matters in a mutually satisfactory compromise, and your vet may be able to advise you as to the best strategy to adopt. Alternatively, there are practitioners who specialize in behavioural problems of companion animals, and a referral to one of these will usually provide the solution to the problem.

### CHAPTER FOUR

# Domestic
# Upheavals

▲ *A cat gazes serenely through the bars of her run at a cattery.*

DOMESTIC UPHEAVALS

▲ *A well designed cattery, with enclosed sleeping accommodation and individual runs.*
◄ *'Were you thinking of packing these books?'*

Cats are creatures of habit, and the best training strategy is one of gentle persuasion into the habits you prefer. When these habits are upset, trouble is liable to follow, and sometimes the actual nature of the problem is unexpected. You should always, therefore, try to think ahead when any domestic upheaval is in the offing, and anticipate what effect the disruption will have on your cat. In this way you can plan your strategy for smoothing things out, and make any necessary arrangements well in advance.

## HOLIDAYS

When you are planning your holiday, remember that your cat, as a member of the family, needs to have arrangements made at the same time. The sudden realization while you are packing that you have not organized the feline vacation – or even a safe parking place – can lead to some tricky situations.

■ **BOARDING CATTERIES** Without a doubt a good boarding cattery is the easiest and safest solution to the holiday problem. However, there are poorly run catteries as well as good ones, and it is best to take time to assess the facilities of several before making a final choice. The initial elimination can be done by telephone: if the proprietor is unwilling to show you your pet's accommoda-

tion, cross her or him off and try someone else. Another important point is vaccination requirements: a cattery should *insist* that your cat's vaccinations for both feline infectious enteritis and cat flu are complete and up to date. If this subject is not raised without prompting then it maybe that they are not as strict about it as they ought to be, and if it is stated that vaccination is not necessary, then again go elsewhere.

Next you should visit one or two possibilities to check the accommodation. Each cat (or each family's cats, as companions will of course stay together) should have individual accommodation of reasonable size. Small hospital-type cages are much too confining for a healthy cat for more than a day or so. Accommodation may be entirely indoors or there may be a smaller inside living area with an adjoining outside run. Wire mesh enclosures to the runs are perfectly acceptable, and many cats like to watch all the comings and goings and the other residents, but it should be possible for him to retreat into his own safe inside space whenever he wants to. The sleeping area should be raised off the floor, and there should be provision for heating. Also provided should be clean comfortable bedding, clean food and water dishes, a litter tray, a scratching post (or the wooden supports of the run) and perhaps a few toys. However, your cat will settle in better if you take some familiar belongings, such as his bed or favourite toys, and leave these with it. As an extra treat, you might also leave a garment of your own, such as an old woollen sweater – it is surprising how much this will help to prevent him from feeling abandoned.

Enquire also about food. Many cats have strong likes and dislikes even among canned foods, and all good catteries make an effort to ensure that your pet's diet is not disrupted along with the rest of his routine. A final point concerns veterinary attention. You should satisfy yourself that arrangements for summoning and paying for any necessary veterinary attention are adequate. Many catteries prefer to stick exclusively to their own vet, and usually this arrangement is quite sufficient, but if your cat suffers from chronic ailment or is convalescing, and your own vet is reasonably local, you may prefer to insist that he or she is the one who is called if necessary. Indeed, if you are concerned on this point, it may be advisable to enquire of your own vet whether he or she attends any catteries, and whether they would recommend any of them (this does not necessarily follow!), and use this as a basis for choosing.

Once you have selected the Hilton in which your cat will reside in luxury during your absence, the most important task is to make sure his vaccination status is adequate. If he has not been vaccinated previously against cat flu, you will have to arrange for the course to be started at least six weeks before you are due to leave. After that, all that remains is to deliver him to the cattery with appropriate 'security blankets' and vaccination certificate, and if you plan an early start this is best done the day before. It is also a good idea to do a quick once-over with flea-spray just before this, to avoid any embarrassing revelations at the cattery and to give some protection against any he may encounter while there (another dose on return will not go amiss either). Try to avoid prolonged farewells – after all, it is only for a week or two – and do not worry about pining. You may find that he has eaten less than usual while in the cattery, but will soon make up for it once home, and the most common problem when picking up your cat from a good establishment is the horrible, dawning suspicion that your pet has probably had a much better time than you have had!

■ **TAKING YOUR CAT ON VACATION.** The feasibility of this plan depends partly on the sort of holiday you plan, but also to a great extent on the character and temperament of your cat. Person-oriented cats will always cope with this much better than territory-oriented ones.

The idea of taking your cat on a foreign holiday is probably not one you should consider. Quarantine laws are the major problem: any cat taken out of the British Isle to *any* other country, even for a few days or even minutes, will be subject to six months (expensive) anti-rabies quarantine on return, and no cat may be taken into Britain, no matter for how short a stay, without passing through the same quarantine period; Hawaii also requires cats from countries where rabies is present to undergo four months of quarantine, and this *includes cats from the Mainland;* and Australia and New Zealand jointly do not accept cats from anywhere but the British Isles, and even then quarantine is required. Even where no quarantine is necessary there may be requirements for specific vaccinations and import procedures which would also be applied to a cat accompanying a holiday-maker.

For the holiday 'at home', however, the main consideration is the nature of the accommodation. Certain types of variations are obviously out of the question, such as bus tours and hiking expeditions, but with others arrangements are possible. Be sure to enquire of your hotel in good time, as it is really not on simply to turn up complete with cat and expect to be welcome. However, many hotels are surprisingly ready to accept pets, on condition they are kept under control and do not disturb other residents or staff. With a cat, this usually means confining him to your room, which has the merit of being a safe place, but you should consider whether the onset of extreme boredom might signal some embarrassing behaviour. Hotels which refuse pets usually do so because of bad experiences in the past, and if your cat destroys the upholstery, shreds the wallpaper and leaves a puddle in the middle of the carpet the next person who enquires about bringing one is liable to receive a very short answer! Self-catering holidays (rental cottages and the like) are generally easier, but here the question arises as to whether the cat should be allowed outside. Provided your pet is the unexcitable laid-back type who has shown that he can be trusted in a strange place, and the area is free from particular dangers such as busy road, this is probably reasonable, but a nervous, highly strung cat should not be taken on holiday unless you are sure that he can be kept safely indoors.

If you do decide on a 'cat comes too' holiday, remember that you will also have to pack for him. You will need to take food and water bowls, enough food for the first day or two, his bed or a reasonable substitute, and a litter tray, scoop and litter. Even when a cat who normally goes outside is taken on holiday with access to a garden a litter tray is a good idea in case he is intimidated by the strange surroundings outside. For a hotel stay extra items will be necessary – a can-opener, and a spoon or fork for dishing food out, also a blanket to protect the hotel's bedspread, as it is unlikely that you will be able to prevent your cat from sleeping on the bed. Remember also some newspaper, plastic bags and sellotape (scotch tape), as soiled cat litter can be disposed of in a wastepaper basket provided it is well wrapped in newspaper and sealed in a plastic bag. A small brush and dustpan are also very use-

▲ *Open cupboards and fragile ornaments are tempting fate when there is a cat in the house.*

▲ *Cats and dogs need not be enemies – this red tabby is clearly not in the least alarmed by the terrier.*

ful for tidying up stray granules, especially if the tray is placed on a tiled bathroom floor. When you leave, make sure that all traces of feline presence have been erased, and be particularly generous when thanking the chamber-maid.

■ **LEAVING YOUR CAT AT HOME.** This strategy relies on the cooperation of friends or neighbours, and is often deemed suitable because cats are seen as territorial and not much concerned with the identity of the person wielding the can-opener. This is certainly the case with some cats, but a number of people do not actually realize just how at-tracted their cats are to them personally until they are surprised by the bad reaction to their absence. It is very risky indeed to allow a cat to roam while you are away, and puts a very great responsibility on the person feeding him. At the very least he should have access to home via a cat flap, but even so it is quite possible that he will take off across town in search of you. It is better if he can be kept and fed indoors, which means your friend will have to attend to a litter tray as well as to meals, and take great care to avoid any chance of an escape. Better still if your cat-sitter can have your cat to stay in his or her own house, confined indoors, as a cat who perceives himself as living with someone, especially someone you approve of, is much less likely to disappear than one who is being fed in an empty house. Make sure that your cat-sitter has your holiday address, and the name and phone number of your veterinary surgeon.

■ **PREPARING FOR A MOVE.** Cats just *love* boxes. And cabinets and cupboards. And bits of string, balls of news-paper and piles of clean sheets. Packing is therefore going to provide much more fun for your cat, and the greatest fun is being a real pest and watching you lose your temper. The way round this is to tackle your packing in rooms which are definitely out of bounds, and to en-sure that all boxes, cupboards and so on are shut before he is allowed back in again. Be sure to leave the cat's own things – bed, food bowl, toys – until the very last minute, so that the chance of his becoming upset enough either to vanish or to display some antisocial behaviour is mini-mized. Even previously well-trained cats may start spray-marking if they feel that their territory is being seriously disrupted or threatened, and packing antics which began as a game may end up as a real behavioural problem.

■ **THE DAY OF THE MOVE.** When a cat senses a really major disruption happening around him, his most usual reaction is simply to remove himself from it as quickly and effec-tively as he can. On the day of the move your main aim is therefore to ensure that when the moment comes to pack the cat is actually available to be packed, rather than delaying the move by hours while you comb the neigh-bourhood. It is best to keep him shut in one room, with food and litter tray, and when the time comes to empty that room, to move him to one which has already been cleared. In this way you can postpone putting him in the basket until the last moment, and if you are making a number of back and forth trips you should only take him with the final load.

At the other end it is even more important to follow this procedure in reverse. Again confining the cat to one room with food and litter tray, and get on with organizing the house. When you have one room reasonably organized (but also reasonably cat-proof) you can move him to deal with the first room. In this way you can ensure that the first introduction to the new home is in the evening, when things have stabilized and the frenetic upheaval has subsided. This will help to avoid negative or unpleasant associations with the new house. If you are really worried that your cat will be seriously upset by the business of moving it may be a good idea to consider leaving him at a cattery for a few days while you sort yourself out.

■ **IN THE NEW HOME.** The speed with which you can allow your cat free run of the house and then the garden will depend very much on individual character. Some cats will instantly settle in anywhere where their favourite people are, with no problems at all. More nervous cats will require a gentle introduction to the great outdoors, and perhaps will have to be introduced to a large house in gradual stages. If you sense that trouble may be brew-ing, return to the strategy you originally used to intro-duce him to home. It should be easier this time, as the people and furnishings are familiar, but do make sure that the address on the collar tag is up to date before you finally let him loose, just in case.

You may be concerned by stories of cats who refuse to accept a family move and repeatedly, inexplicably, keep returning to their previous home. However, this sort of occurrence is actually rare, and few cats are so extremely territory-oriented. If you treat the introduction to his new home with tact and care there is every prospect that your cat will settle in well, and many cats have accompanied their owners to a succession of different homes with no problems whatsoever.

## ADDITIONS TO THE FAMILY

Cats can become surprisingly jealous of their people and their territory, and can react badly to the discovery that they are now sharing either of these with someone else. A cat with wounded feelings is not nice to live with – a profound and prolonged sulk may be the least of the problems, and antisocial behaviour such as territory spraying and even aggression can develop. It is therefore

**DOMESTIC UPHEAVALS**

in everyone's interest to be particularly tender of the cat's feelings when new members are added to a family.

■ **ADULTS.** Few problems need be anticipated when, for example, elderly parents come to join an already large family. The main problem is usually when a cat which has been the sole companion of a single man or woman suddenly realizes that there is now someone else to contend with. This is best tackled by the new person making particular efforts to make friends with the cat. 'Love me, love my pet' applies just as much to cats as to dogs. After the upheaval of wedding/honeymoon/new house is over, both partners should make a point of making a fuss of the cat, petting and playing with him and generally making him feel wanted. The chances are he will soon realize that having two people to be spoiled rotten by is even better than one.

■ **NEW BABIES.** If cats may sometimes be jealous of adult interlopers, this is nothing to what can happen when something human, but cat-sized and pampered just like a cat, suddenly appears on the scene. All of a sudden the parents have much less time for the cat and the baby is getting all the attention. Try to appreciate the cat's feelings and however tired you are, spare some time to make a fuss of him and spoil him a little. Introduce him carefully to the baby, to satisfy his curiosity, but be sure not to leave them alone together. It is rare for a cat to attack a baby, but there is a danger that he will try to settle down in the pram (carriage), cot or crib, drawn by the warmth of the baby. Again, he is unlikely to lie over the baby's face, but if a heavy cat lies over a baby's chest then the baby may be unable to breathe against the weight, and this is probably the commonest cause of tragedies with babies involving cats. If you do have to leave the baby where the cat might have access, you should fit some kind of net or other cover which is fixed to prevent a cat actually getting into the pram (carriage), crib or playpen, and which will not allow his weight to fall on the baby. As the baby grows, dangers of this sort disappear, and the different problems of integrating toddlers with cats will arise. However, most sensible cats adjust to children as they grow, and come to some sort of mutual non-aggression pact. Children must also be taught to handle animals properly. Once beyond the toddler stage they will form their own relationships with pets, which will enhance their experience and enrich their lives as they grow.

■ **OTHER PETS.** When you acquire smaller pets such as rodents, birds or fish the main problem is simply to arrange their accommodation to ensure that there is no

▶ *Even unrelated cats of different ages can grow to be inseparable companions.*

DOMESTIC UPHEAVALS

▲ *The yellow Labradors and the British Blue seem to be involved in a conspiracy to occupy the best sofa.*

chance of their becoming a feline lunch. Some cats make gerbil-watching a hobby so a very strong case is essential, one which cannot be knocked over or opened and will not come apart. The real question of peaceful coexistence comes when a dog or another cat joins the family, and again the degree of trouble which arises depends largely on the character of your cat. Some will accept and make friends with the newcomer very quickly while others are extremely resentful. Strangely, other cats or kittens may be more of a problem than dogs. An established cat often has little difficulty dominating a new puppy, and even an adult dog, so long as it is not a cat-chaser, may soon be tolerated. One thing which needs care, however, is food. If the cat is not used to gobbling his whole meal the instant it is served, he may well go hungry, as dogs find cat food quite delicious – it is best to find somewhere to place the cat's food dish which is not accessible to the dog. A cat's most extreme reaction to an interloper is to leave home, which is usually in response to the acquisition of a new kitten. It is therefore important to be aware of this possibility when expanding the feline population and to be prepared for a lengthy period of adjustment. You may have to confine both cats indoors for some time until first tolerance then friendship have built up, and quite close supervision will be needed to ensure that squabbles and disagreements do not extend to full-scale warefare. Be particularly attentive to your long-standing pet during

this time – single him out for special petting, and do not be afraid to spoil him a little. There is a real danger of a once-placid house cat turning into a harried unkempt stray who only appears about once a week to snatch some food if this period of adjustment is not carefully handled. However, even the most sulky, resentful cats do come round in the end, and you will know you have succeeded when you find both cats in a corner of the garden plotting how to get the best sleeping-place in the house.

## EMERGENCIES

When something goes disastrously wrong in the family, do try not to forget the cat, who does not understand about car accidents or sudden illness. Somebody will at least have to feed him. A friendly neighbour who can be telephoned in cases of dire emergency, and who has access to a spare key, is invaluable. If continuing disruption is likely, a cattery stay may be indicated. The single person should take particular thought about accidents. Cards are available which can be kept beside an organ donor card to inform emergency services that you have a pet who may be shut in at home. Your own name and address, and the name and address of a friend who has previously agreed to see to your cat in an emergency should be written clearly, and the card should be carried at all times.

## CHAPTER FIVE

# Breeding

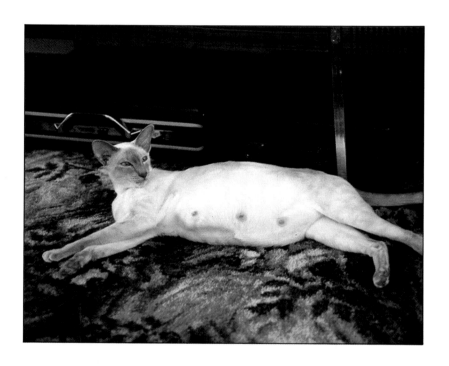

▲ *This heavily pregnant queen is the picture of confidence and contentment.*

## DECIDING TO HAVE A LITTER

Cats are, of course, adorable, and kittens especially so. However, there are many more cats around at the present time than there are homes to care for them, as any cat sanctuary organizer will tell you, and it is very important to consider whether you are absolutely sure that you will be able to find caring permanent homes for the kittens before deciding to breed. If you are not sure (and remember that even friends sometimes change their minds, or return a kitten or throw him out of the house if problems develop), and you cannot keep the kittens yourself, then it would be better to have your queen spayed. If you do decide to breed then it is important to wait until your queen is at least a year old before mating, so that she has finished growing herself. It is also advisable for the sake of her health to limit pregnancies to one per year.

## CHOOSING A TOM

Cats have no paternity rights, and if you want kittens you must therefore first own an entire (unspayed) queen, then choose a suitable husband for her if you want to be sure of the pedigree of the kittens. Among non-pedigrees, matings are seldom deliberately arranged. The usual method of organizing a mating is simply to leave the door open when the queen is calling, and let her and the local toms sort it out among themselves. Many truly gorgeous kittens have originated in this way, and the uncertainty can add to the fun of watching the kittens grow. This does rather depend on there being at least one entire tom in the neighbourhood, but in spite of neutering campaigns and even simple common sense, this is nearly always the case, and few queens who escape when calling fail to become pregnant.

If you have a pedigree queen you will of course want to choose a mate for her, of her own breed. The usual strategy is to choose one whose particularly good points are her less good features, and if you are inexperienced it is advisable to consult an experienced breeder of your particular breed for advice. Closely related toms should be avoided unless you are following a deliberate line-breeding programme. Your queen will have to stay with the tom for several days, and you should be aware that in addition to up-to-date vaccination for both FIE and cat flu, all reputable breeders will insist that visiting queens are certified negative for feline leukaemia virus (FeLV) infection on a blood test. Your vet will be able to arrange this for you.

## MATING

The usual procedure for arranged matings is to take the queen to the tom's home as soon as she is observed to begin calling, and to leave her there until the period of oestrus (heat) is over. However, some queens require the stimulus of a tom's presence to bring them into heat, and in these cases it may be necessary to leave the queen with the tomcat and simply wait for her to begin calling. This requires careful handling, as a tom may react aggressively towards a strange, non-receptive female, and it is wise to be sure that the breeder who owns the tom is capable and experienced before trusting your queen to him or her.

Mating in cats is quite a violent affair, with a lot of yelling, growling and tail-lashing and so on. When the tom mounts the queen he stabilizes himself by taking a firm grip on the scruff of her neck, and it is not unusual for a queen to lose large chunks of fur from her ruff! Conversely, some passionate queens have been known to chew parts of the tom's fur almost bald.

Cats have absolutely no concept of marital fidelity, and it is quite possible, even likely if the opportunity arises,

## MATING IN THE CAT

Mating in the cat. In pedigree matings such as this one the event usually takes place in the tom's home. Note the firm grip the tom has taken of the queen's scruff. Because of the association of sex with biting, an excited cat may sometimes forget himself and bite (or scratch) at inappropriate moments, gaining an undeserved reputation for treachery and viciousness.

## PARTURITION IN THE CAT

Cats normally give birth without any difficulty. The first signs that a queen is about to give birth include general restlessness and heaving movements of her flanks, indicating that contractions have begun. At this point, she should be confined to the room where the nesting box is located (**1**). After a period of straining, the first kitten will appear as a protrusion from the vagina. Once the kitten is born, the mother will free it from any retaining membranes and rupture the umbilical cord (**2**). Most will be born at regular intervals (**3**) and each one will be licked vigorously to encourage it to breathe (**4**). After each kitten is born, its placenta or afterbirth will be passed and the mother may eat it if it is not taken away (**5**). It is important to check that one afterbirth has been passed for each kitten. The kittens may begin sucking before the last of the litter is born (**6**); once all the kittens have arrived, the mother will settle and clean them thoroughly while they feed (**7**). Most litters consist of about four kittens.

BREEDING

for a queen to mate with two, three or more toms during the oestrus period. Consequently, kittens born in the same litter can have different fathers, a phenomenon which goes a long way to explaining the random assortment of colours in some non-pedigree litters. If there is any doubt whatsoever about the paternity of even one of the kittens in a 'pedigree' litter it is likely that the owner of the tom will refuse to allow any of the litter to be registered as that tom's progeny. This is the main reason for requiring a queen to stay with the chosen tom until she has passed completely out of heat – the other being that if she is mated several times the litter size is likely to be larger than from a single mating.

## GESTATION

Pregnancy in the cat lasts for about nine weeks. During the first three weeks there is very little to see, although some queens occasionally seem slightly unwell. At about three weeks of pregnancy you may notice the queen's nipples appearing pinker than usual, especially if this is her first litter. By about the fifth week your vet will be able to detect the growing kittens by abdominal palpation, and during the last third of pregnancy you may observe the queen's abdomen becoming noticeably larger. In the last couple of weeks she will often seem restless, and will prowl around the house searching for a good nest for the kittens.

The most important matter in the care of the pregnant queen is diet. She will require a normal, high-protein, well-balanced diet during the first five or six weeks, but during the last third of pregnancy when the kittens are growing rapidly she will need considerably more, perhaps half as much again depending on appetite. Extra calcium tablets and cod liver oil to provide vitamins are also advisable at this stage. It is also beneficial to treat her for roundworms about five weeks after mating to reduce the level of infection which the kittens will be exposed to, and if she was not given a booster vaccination before mating then one given during pregnancy (your vet will use only dead vaccines at this stage) will improve the level of protection which will be passed on to the kittens. Otherwise, simply take care when handling your queen not to put excessive pressure on her abdomen, and allow her to take as much exercise as she wants, in order to keep her muscles in good condition.

## PARTURITION

When you see your queen beginning to search for a nesting place, it is time to provide her with a kittening

◄ *This lilac point Siamese looks very placid with her nursing litter, but the glint in her eye is a warning not to approach much nearer.*

▲ *These growing kittens are getting rather large for their mother to cope with – soon they will be weaned on to solid food.*

box of your choosing and to encourage her to use it. Custom-made kittening cages are available which can be secured against invaders, and these are possibly advisable if there are other cats in the household who might disturb the mother and family. However, in a single cat home a large cardboard box makes a perfectly acceptable substitute. Paper is a better bed than blankets, both because it is more easily disposable and because kittens are much less likely to become dangerously entangled. It is also advisable to arrange the lid or cover so that you can look in on the queen and check how things are progressing.

In the last day or so before the birth you will see milk in the queen's teats. The first signs of labour are increased restlessness, frequent visits to the litter tray, and nervous last-minute rearrangement of the nest. When things start to happen in earnest you may notice panting, loud purring or occasional crying, followed by the onset of abdominal contractions and straining. The first kitten will usually be born within half an hour, followed by the remainder of the litter over the next three or four hours, although sometimes there is a much longer gap after the first one or two kittens. Each kitten will appear in a fluid-filled sac, which usually bursts during or immediately after the birth, and as soon as the kitten is born the queen will lick it vigorously to stimulate breathing, and bite through the umbilical cord. A placenta (afterbirth) will be passed for each kitten, usually only a few minutes later, but you may miss this as it is the queen's normal instinct to eat all the membranes and placentas. When all the kittens have been delivered the queen will allow them to suckle, and the whole family will often settle down quietly and go to sleep.

Most cats cope perfectly well with labour on their own, and it is seldom necessary to call in veterinary help. However, you should alert your vet as to when the birth is expected so that an emergency will not take her or him completely by surprise, and if you are inexperienced then be sure to discuss the danger signs to be alert for. Queens vary as to whether they prefer isolation or to have a paw held during the whole process, and you should play this by ear using the knowledge of your pet's character. However, do try to observe that the membranes are broken on each kitten as soon as it is born, or it may drown, and be prepared to do this yourself and dry the kitten by brisk rubbing with a towel if the queen does not seem to know how to do this. Also, try to check that the number of placentas equals the number of kittens, as a retained placenta will cause the queen to become very sick.

## LACTATION

During the time when a queen is suckling her litter she requires very large amounts of food indeed – up to *four*

## NATURAL REARING

Small kittens require the stimulus of their mother's tongue in order to urinate and defaecate – she keeps the nest clean by consuming the urine and faeces until the kittens are old enough to use a litter tray. When kittens are being hand reared it is most important to mimic this function with damp cotton wool.

*times* her normal intake – and it is best to feed her, on demand, as much as she seems to want to eat. She will stay with her kittens constantly during the first couple of days, so food and a litter tray should be placed within very easy reach of the nest. During the first two or three weeks it is important to keep the room where the brood is living at a constant high temperature, or to provide a special source of heat, as kittens can easily develop hypothermia. During this time the kittens are completely dependent on their mother. Their only nourishment is her milk, and they require the stimulus of her licking to pass urine and faeces, which she will clean up. However, after about three weeks the kittens' eyes will be open, they will be taking an interest in the outside world, and trying their first experimental laps at their mother's food dish. From this time she will begin to encourage them to use the litter tray, and it is very important to ensure that the height of the sides of the tray and its position are not such as to prevent a tiny kitten clambering in or out. An easily accessible litter tray at this stage generally eliminates any need for human toilet training.

## HAND-REARING

Hand-rearing of kittens is a very tricky subject. One would expect that hand-reared kittens would be particularly friendly and sociable, as are hand-reared calves and lambs, but this is not the case. Deprived of a feline social

BREEDING

education from their mothers, such kittens are usually cranky, maladjusted, unpleasant individuals, sometimes downright vicious. It is therefore much preferable to arrange a foster mother if at all possible for rejected kittens or those who have lost their mother. However, hand-rearing is certainly possible and commercial cat's milk substitutes are available from pet shops and vets, along with suitable feeding bottles or syringes. Milk should be fed at 98.4°F (37°C), giving very small amounts (5–10ml) every two to three hours, day and night. As the kittens grow, the size of the feeds can be increased and the intervals between them lengthened; after three weeks the night feeds can be discontinued. Great care must be taken to keep orphan kittens warm, for example a heating pad or infra-red lamp, and it is important to keep them clean and to stimulate urination and defaecation by massaging the abdomen and under the tail with slightly damp cotton wool after each feed. After six to eight weeks these kittens can be weaned in the same way as normally-reared kittens.

## WEANING AND HOMING

It is advisable to start touting your kittens' charms round all your friends and acquaintances just as soon as their eyes open and they start to look marketably cute. It is a great advantage to have all the kittens spoken for well in advance, but you should still insist that your victims wait until their future lords and masters are at least eight weeks old before they take them home. Be careful, however, to check the suitability of all prospective new owners, and satisfy yourself that a good home is really being offered before you agree to let anyone have a kitten.

From about three weeks old, kittens will begin to show an interest in solid food, and you can begin to offer small amounts of cat's milk substitute, baby cereal or baby food. Over the next three weeks their consumption will increase, as the queen progressively allows them to nurse less and less. At about six weeks old the kittens can be introduced to actual cat food, which ought to be a canned variety at first, and preferably a specially formulated kitten food. By eight weeks of age the kittens should be eating enough to be fully independent of their mother, and it is best to arrange for them to move to their new homes as soon as possible after this, as prolonged nursing by large growing kittens can drain a queen considerably and cause her to become quite debilitated. Newly weaned kittens should be given four meals per day for the first couple of months, then the meals can gradually be reduced until by six months old the kitten is being fed in the routine which it is intended to follow when adult.

▶ *This basketful is completely irresistable – but do make sure that prospective new owners really want and can care for a growing cat.*

CHAPTER SIX

# The Sick or Injured Cat

▲ *A veterinary surgeon examines a cat's ear using an auriscope.*

## RECOGNIZING WHEN YOUR CAT IS UNWELL

If your cat becomes ill it is unnecessary, and almost always counter-productive, to try to diagnose the illness yourself. It is most probable that you will cause yourself unnecessary worry by imagining serious diseases which are in fact out of the question, but there is also a very real danger that you will be lulled into a false sense of security by mistaking a major illness for a minor one, and perhaps fail to seek help in time. It is much more important to be able simply to recognize when there is something significantly amiss with your cat and to seek veterinary attention promptly.

One important general point: on no account must painkillers for humans be fed to cats, as these, especially aspirin and paracetamol, are poisonous to them.

■ **PHYSICAL SIGNS.** These include lumps, cuts, runny eyes, scabs, weight loss, evidence of pain and anything else which seems abnormal on examination of the cat. The maintenance of a regular grooming routine really proves its value in this area. Firstly, it enables you to become familiar with your cat's body so that you know what is normal – it is not uncommon for unobservant owners suddenly to notice some innocuous feature such as a mat of hair or the area of sparse coat above the eyes, and rush to the vet in a panic. This is not only embarrassing, but expensive. Secondly, the regular close examination of the cat allows you to notice abnormalities when they occur and to seek help at an early stage. If you are able to point clearly to a physical abnormality and state accurately when this first appeared and how it has been progressing, then the vet's task of diagnosis is very much easier.

■ **BEHAVIOURAL SIGNS.** These can be more difficult to define than physical signs, as their recognition depends on your observation that the cat is not behaving in his normal way. This may involve such things as a refusal to eat, excessive drinking, a reduction in his usual level of playfulness, frequent recourse to the litter tray or behaviour suggestive of discomfort somewhere in the body. Of course, such things will normally alter with time and the normal ageing process, but changes of this sort are usually very gradual and any sudden change is a matter for concern. When your main reason for consulting your vet is the observation of worrying behavioural signs it is particularly important to be able to give an accurate account of your observations, as it may be that even the vet can find little which is abnormal on clinical examination and his or her diagnosis must be based to a large extent on your account of the problem. Even the decision as to which laboratory tests or X-rays may be needed requires some sort of first guess about what might be wrong, which again must be based on your observations. It sometimes happens that a particularly alert owner will recognize behavioural changes in the very early stages of serious disease, but that the vet is unable to find anything wrong simply because the disease is not yet advanced enough to allow any recognizable physical signs to be seen. The cat may well have to be sent away at this stage with no or only palliative treatment. However, should the signs persist or become worse, you must not hesitate to pay a second visit, as by this stage clearly identifiable diagnostic abnormalities may have become evident.

## THE SKIN

Being superficial, skin disorders are among the easiest of conditions to recognize. Some owners are rather repelled by the idea of a skin condition but skin disease is rarely very serious or life-threatening and successful treatment is quite usual. Physical signs to look for are patches of bare skin or thin or broken hair, crusts or scabs, and a reddened or blackened appearance on the skin. Behavioural signs such as scratching or pulling at the hair are usually but not always present.

By far the most common cause of skin problems in cats is flea infestation. Some cats are violently allergic to fleas and come up in an acute skin reaction to only a few bites, while others may be absolutely alive with parasites while showing few signs. The majority of animals politely diagnosed as having 'hormonal imbalance' do seem to recover miraculously when strict flea control is instituted. This is therefore a reasonable first line of attack when a cat which is otherwise well develops an itchy, scabby skin. Fleas spend at least 90 per cent of their time not on the cat but in the cat's bedding, only hopping on occasionally for a meal. Of the two-pronged attack on the parasite, therefore, control of the cat's environment is the more important. Here the choice is between spray organochlorine/ganophosphorous insecticides which are applied every two to three months, and a powder preparation which destroys the flea population by preventing them from breeding. The latter is much slower to come to its full effect but has the advantage of being non-toxic. For control of the fleas on the cat a spray preparation containing dichlorvos, used every two weeks, is by far the most effective against an established heavy infestation, but a flea collar renewed frequently in accordance with the manufacturer's instructions may be adequate simply to prevent a clean cat from picking up the odd flea. However, the spray and the collar are *alternatives* – both contain powerful insecticides, and the use of a flea spray or powder on a cat wearing a flea collar may add up to a poisonous dose for the cat. Note also that flea collars themselves irritate the skin of some cats.

▲ *This odd-eyed white may well be deaf in one ear, but it would be very difficult to be sure of this.*

If a skin problem in a cat persists in spite of adequate flea control, or is accompanied by other signs of ill health, or appears very raw and 'weepy' rather than dry and scabby, then it is essential to seek veterinary advice. There is a very large number of other skin conditions which affect cats (a few of which are transmissible to humans) and it is almost impossible for a cat owner to distinguish between them.

## THE EARS

As well as becoming involved with an extensive flea in-festation, the ears host their own parasite, the ear mite. Cats with ear mites scratch their ears almost constantly, often making the ear flap very sore, and have a dark, gritty discharge in the ear. Treatment is usually straightforward, so long as you take care to ensure that the ear drops do go right down inside the ear, but some cats are subject to recurrent attacks. It is important to have conditions like this seen to promptly, as chronically inflamed ears can be very difficult to treat, sometimes requiring surgery, and persistent scratching may cause a blood blister (haema-toma) of the ear flap which again will require surgery.

Deafness in cats is most often a congenital condition associated with a pure white coat and blue eyes. Odd-eyed whites with one blue eye are sometimes deaf in one ear. If you are considering buying a blue-eyed white kitten, be sure to test his hearing before parting with any money, as this condition is incurable. Older cats occasionally become deaf with advancing years, and again there is little effective treatment. Deaf cats should only be allowed outdoors under very close supervision because of the danger from traffic, and you will have to devise a system for attracting such a cat's attention visually.

## THE EYES

A wide variety of conditions can affect the eyes, and a number of different signs may be visible. A watery or pussy discharge in both eyes is frequently a sign of cat flu, while one eye which is screwed tight shut and dripping tears may have an injury to the eyeball or an object trapped behind the eyelids (often a grass seed), or perhaps both. Protrusion of the third eyelids (haws) half-way across the eyes frequently accompanies general ill health in a cat, and is not really specifically indicative of any one condition or indeed of anything actually wrong with the eyes themselves.

Blindness in cats is fairly uncommon. There may be physical evidence of an eye abnormality such as opacity of the transparent cornea on the front of the eye or a cloudiness deeper within the eye, but the eyes of some blind cats look perfectly normal, and behavioural signs such as walking into objects or the apparent inability to see a food dish may be the only clues. Another suspicious pointer is when the black pupils of the eyes remain wide open instead of contracting to slits in bright light. Certain conditions causing blindness may be amenable to surgery, but even where treatment is not possible blind cats usually cope remarkably well. Where only one eye is affected it may cause very little inconvenience. Even complete blindness is usually compensated for by acute hearing and careful use of the tactile whiskers, and so long as the positions of the furniture are not changed a great deal most cats will live a reasonably contented life.

## THE URINARY SYSTEM

Kidney failure is an extremely common condition in the cat. As it mostly affects elderly cats it is discussed in detail in Chapter 7, but it can occur at any age. The main early warning sign is a gradual increase in the cat's water consumption, often accompanied by loss of weight. It is important not to restrict the water intake no matter how much the cat is drinking, and to obtain veterinary advice. There are in fact a number of other causes of excessive thirst which must be considered, such as diabetes and hepatitis, and correct diagnosis is important before specific treatment can be initiated.

Cats are also rather prone to the development of bladder stones. In the female, these are passed out with little trouble, but they can become stuck in the narrower urinary passage of the male and cause a blockage. This is known as feline urological syndrome, or FUS. Signs are frequent non-productive straining in the litter tray, often accompanied by crying, and frequent licking of the end of the penis. This condition can be serious and cause cats to become very ill, and it is essential to seek veterinary help within a few hours of the signs being noticed. Surgical removal of the blockage is often successful, but the condition tends to recur and a special diet may be prescribed to prevent this. It is unwise to feed dry cat food to a cat with a tendency to FUS.

## POISONING

Cats tend to scavenge indiscriminately less than dogs, and so suffer from poisoning less often, but it is still a possibility to be borne in mind. Signs of poisoning vary depending on the actual poison involved, and can be very similar to the signs of infectious disease with the exception that fever is unusual and hypothermia more common.

There are three main classes of signs: nervous signs such as fits, tremors and excessive salivation; coma; and uncontrollable bleeding. Nervous signs are usually caused by insecticides or weedkillers (and this includes most of the drugs used for flea control, which can cause poisoning if used incorrectly). Coma is produced by the rat poison alphachloralose, and uncontrollable bleeding is caused by the rat poison Warfarin and its derivatives (coumarin-type drugs). Alphachloralose is the least worrying of these poisons as it is only necessary to keep the cat warm until the effects wear off, and if you require a rodent control preparation this is much safer than Warfarin so far as pets are concerned. (Even safer is norbormide – 'Raticate' – which is completely non-poisonous to cats or dogs.) Warfarin poisoning usually occurs when a cat eats a mouse or rat which has eaten the poison. It can be very serious, but there is a specific antidote, and the sooner this can be administered the better, as blood transfusion, often required in advanced cases, it not easy in cats due to the difficulty of collecting blood from a donor. Specific antidotes are also available for many of the poisons causing nervous signs, and again any suspicion that your cat has been poisoned should be regarded as an emergency as the earlier the antidote can be administered, the better. Cats which may have been poisoned should be kept very warm and very quiet, and handled as little as possible. It is usually unwise to try to induce vomiting. You should contact your vet as a matter of urgency, and try to make enquiries as to what poisons your cat may have had access to.

## INFECTIOUS DISEASES

There are many different infectious diseases which may affect cats. In general, infections are accompanied by listlessness, a loss of appetite and a reduction in grooming. You may see discharge at the eyes and/or nose, and there may be diarrhoea, vomiting or noisy, laboured breathing. It is not easy to take a cat's temperature accurately, as the insertion of a thermometer into the rectum is tricky and uncomfortable due to the cat's small size, and other

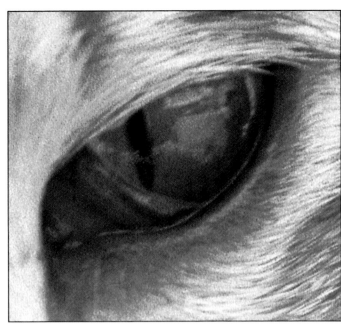

▲ *Protrusion of the third eyelid is a sign of general ill health in a cat.* ▶

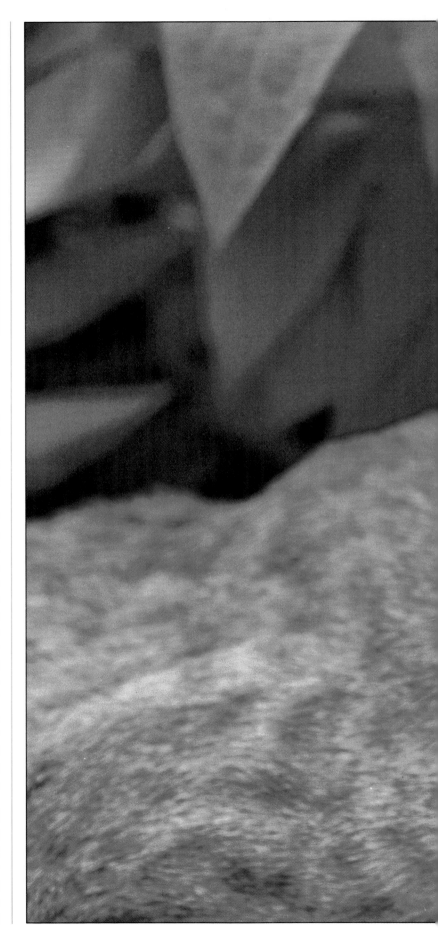

methods do not really give accurate results. However, a fevered cat may feel noticeably hot to the touch and the pads of the feet are often damp and clammy. A cat's normal body temperature is about 101°F (38.3°C) but he would not really be considered to be running a significant temperature until it was over 103°F (39.4°C).

A reasonably comprehensive list of the infectious diseases of the cat and their symptoms would occupy a fairly large textbook, and present space does not even allow the surface of the subject to be scratched. However, as mentioned above, the important thing is not so much to be able to determine that your cat has cat flu, or bronchitis, or hepatitis, but more to recognize that there is something wrong and that it is appropriate to seek veterinary help. You can best assist the vet in diagnosing your pet's illness by being able to describe clearly all that you have observed to be unusual in his appearance or behaviour, say how long this has been apparent, and answer accurately any further questions which your vet may ask. For this reason it is best, if possible, not to send the cat to the vet in the charge of a child or a neighbour, and if it is really impossible for you to go yourself then try to send a concise, comprehensive note detailing everything you think might be significant.

Other than the acute infectious diseases described above, cats are also subject to more chronic, insidious infections. These include feline infectious anaemia, caused by a blood parasite, feline leukaemia, one of the few cancer-type diseases known to be due to an infectious agent, and an immunosuppressive condition known as FTLV which is similar to human AIDS. These conditions

▲ *These two kittens are suffering from a severe dose of cat flu, and are obviously feeling very sorry for themselves.*

usually have a more insidious onset and as the cat's condition deteriorates gradually it can be more difficult to spot that he is actually ill. You should therefore be vigilant for such signs as weight loss, reduced appetite and pallor of the gums, which might be indications of any one of these conditions.

## ZOONOSES

This peculiar word is the term used to refer to diseases which can be passed from animals to people. Much is said and written by ill-informed people about the dangers and health hazards of living with animals, but in fact most infectious diseases limit their virulence to one particular species, and the risks of catching something from a pet are minimal compared to the huge 'danger' of daily contact with other human beings. Nevertheless there are a few particular conditions you should bear in mind which may be transmitted by cats.

■ **TOXOCARIASIS.** is the term used to describe infection by the cat or dog roundworms. It is in fact impossible to catch worms as such from cats with worms, and human worms are either caught directly from other infected humans, or through eating poorly cooked meat which is infected with the larval stage of a human worm. However, the cat roundworm also has a larval stage, and it can happen that this stage infects a human being, a condition known as *visceral larva migrans*. The publicity given to this occurrence vastly outweighs its actual incidence, due mostly to a few cases where a worm larva has damaged an eye, and in any case the dog worm rather than the cat parasite is the most likely offender. However, the possibility of catching this from a cat does exist; the solution is to worm your cat regularly as directed by your vet. Observe strictly the hygiene precautions detailed earlier when handling cat faeces; pregnant women must be especially vigilant, since they are the ones who perhaps would have the most serious repercussions from an infection.

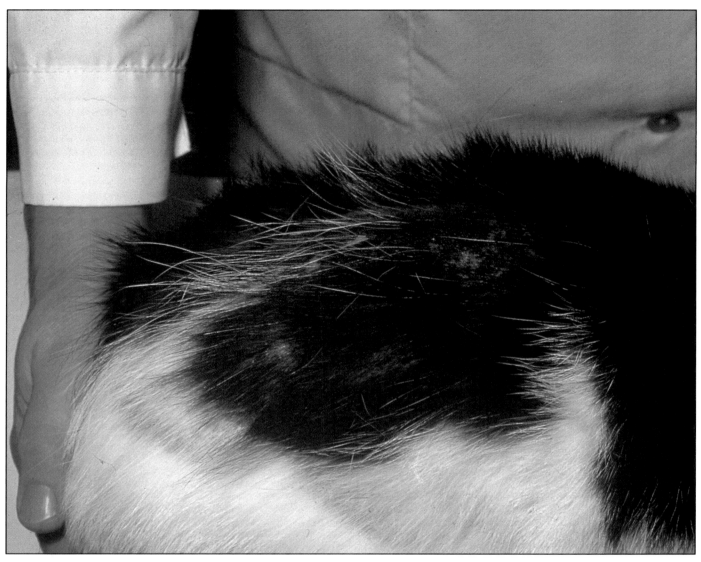

▲ *This cat actually has extensive ringworm, but many different skin conditions may show a very similar appearance.*

■ **TOXOPLASMOSIS.** is caused by a protozoan (single-celled) parasite. This parasite has the cat as its final host but any other species can be infected as an intermediate host. The life cycle of this parasite is very complex, but the main point is that although infection can pass between intermediate hosts by one eating the infected meat of another, only the cat passes out infective stages in its faeces. Acute toxoplasmosis in any species appears as fever, pneumonia and nervous signs, but it is seldom fatal. However, in a pregnant intermediate host the parasite may pass to the foetus and damage it. For this reason pregnant women should *never* handle cat faeces or garden soil where a cat may have defaecated, or tend a litter tray. The other major preventive measure is to avoid feeding raw meat to cats. The chances of infection are again quite small, as infected cats only pass on infection for about two weeks, but due to the potential seriousness of the consequences to an unborn baby, precautions should never be neglected.

■ **RINGWORM.** This disease is not caused by a worm but by a fungus which infects growing hair, and is in many ways very similar to athlete's foot. Cats with ringworm may show patches of baldness with broken hairs, and perhaps rather crusty brown skin, but it is also possible for a cat with ringworm, particularly a longhair, to show no sign of it whatsoever. A vet would be able to diagnose it by laboratory tests. In humans it appears as patches of thickened, reddened skin, often circular, usually on the hands or forearms which are most likely to be in contact with the cat. Very effective drugs are available nowadays to combat ringworm in both cat and human, and in fact the condition is not often particularly serious. It is certainly true that it can sometimes be difficult to eradicate it completely from an infected cat, but there is no reason to follow the reflex reaction of some doctors and have your cat put to sleep just because your child has a patch of ringworm, or at least not without making some attempt to resolve the situation by other means.

THE SICK OR INJURED CAT

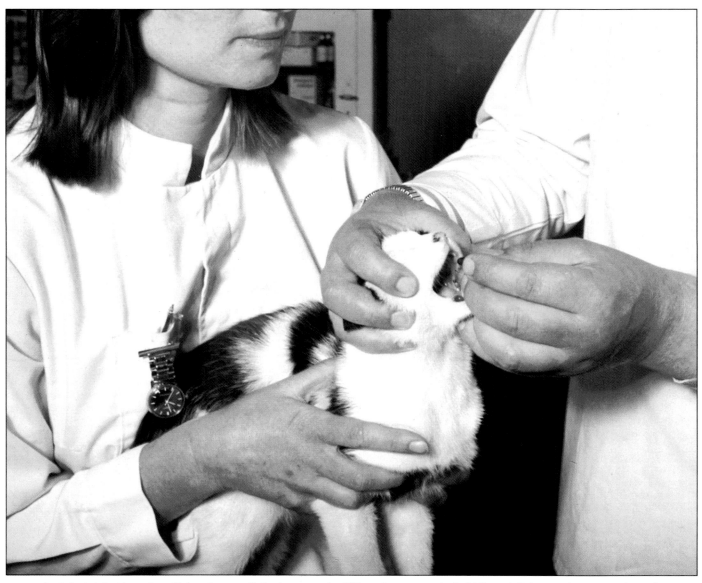

▲ *Administration of medicines by mouth is always easier if there is someone to hold the cat. It is most important to push tablets and capsules right over the back of the tongue.*

## INJURIES AND FIRST AID

The most common causes of injuries in the cat are road accidents and fights. If your cat returns home apparently hurt the easiest way to determine whether he has been hit by a car is to examine his claws, as cats involved in road accidents almost invariably have broken, split claws caused by digging them into the road at the moment of impact. Other signs are fresh dirt in the coat, bleeding from anywhere on the body, pale gums, cold paws and signs of pain. A road accident is most definitely an emergency as even if your cat seems relatively unscathed there may be internal bleeding which you cannot see, and you should contact your veterinary surgeon *at once*. In the meantime keep the cat warm and avoid upsetting him by trying to examine him too closely. If you have to lift him, try to keep the body as flat as possible by supporting it under the shoulders and hips as you lift. If unconscious it is best to transport a cat to the vet lying flat if at all possible. A steady trickle of fairly dark blood is probably not an immediate problem so long as help is sought promptly, but bright spurting blood should be controlled as a matter of urgency – direct pressure on the bleeding point is usually the safest method as tourniquets can be dangerous in unskilled hands. First aid for injuries caused by other means such as falls or domestic accidents follows the same basic principles, but it is surprising how often cats fall quite long distances and completely fail to hurt themselves.

Fight injuries which are large, open gashes may look alarming, but are not usually serious emergencies unless bright spurting blood is seen – a spot of embroidery and a shot of penicillin by the vet the next day is usually all that is required. The more usual fight injury, however, is a bite which leaves only four tiny pinpricks in the skin, but which introduces infection which leads to the development of an abscess. Cats with bite abscesses show pain and an unwillingness to move the affected part, there is often swelling or even a hot, firm lump, and you may be able to feel the tiny bite wounds by gentle probing among the fur. A cat with a bitten paw may be so lame that his owner suspects a broken leg. As the abscess ripens the skin becomes thinner until the whole thing bursts, releasing very nasty pus. This looks alarming, but the cat almost certainly feels better at this stage. Although the lancing of an abscess at the right moment will relieve the pain, this condition is not really an emergency; all but the nastiest cases will clear up very nicely after a few days on penicillin. A burst or lanced abscess should be kept clean by washing with mild antiseptic, and the wound kept open for as long as possible. If a tomcat suffers frequently from bite abscesses you should consider having him neutered.

## NURSING

Surgical or medical treatment given to a sick cat is only half the battle, and high-quality nursing care can make all the difference in speeding your pet along the road to recovery. A sick cat must be kept warm at all times, especially during the night, and an electrically heated pad or an infra-red lamp are invaluable. He should not be expected to go outside to obey the call of nature, but should have a litter tray placed as near his bed as possible. If he cannot walk you may have to carry him to this. It is also important to make him as comfortable as possible, but there may have to be a compromise here between comfort and cleanliness, as where a cat has an unpleasant discharge, or is suffering from vomiting or diarrhoea, it is best to make his bed with something disposable. Old towels and blankets are probably the warmest materials, but newspaper may be quite adequate so long as a good source of heat is provided.

You should make a very positive effort to keep the cat clean, by changing his bedding frequently, wiping his eyes, nose, mouth and under the tail, and sponging soiling from the coat. A fastidious cat who feels too ill to groom itself may become quite depressed if left in a mess, and it is most undesirable for a sick cat to try to clean vomit or diarrhoea from his coat with his tongue. However, try to disturb him as little as possible when you do this.

Encouraging an invalid cat to eat is another important task. Offer him his favourite, tastiest foods, warmed to blood heat to improve acceptability. You may find he will lap but not take solid food, and in this case it is a good idea to put the food through the liquidizer. Alternatively, tinned liquid food for sick cats is available at pet shops.

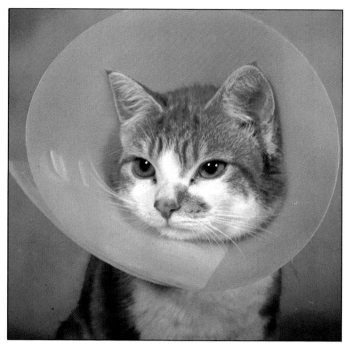

▲ *A well fitted 'Elizabethan Collar'.*

Often when a cat is ill he will not eat directly from a dish but will take food from your fingers – try hand-feeding or simply holding the dish in your hand while he laps. Offer small amounts fairly frequently, and never leave stale food in his dish, which should be thoroughly washed after every meal.

Be very conscientious about administering all medical treatments exactly as instructed by your veterinary surgeon. In particular appreciate the importance of completing a full course of tablets, not just stopping when the cat seems a little better. Ointments and drops are not usually much trouble to apply, though special measures may have to be taken to stop a cat licking off an ointment or otherwise interfering with an injury. The usual method is an 'Elizabethan collar', a wide plastic contraption which is laced on to the cat's own collar and prevents either licking a wound or scratching at an ear or an eye.

Giving tablets to a cat can be very tricky. It is best to hold it between your knees on the floor and open his mouth as described in Chapter 2, and use the forefinger of your left hand to push the pill right over the back of his tongue. Close his mouth, still holding his nose pointed slightly upwards, wait for a few seconds, then open it again. If the pill has not disappeared, it will often do so when you close the cat's mouth a second time. Liquids should be given using a 5ml syringe and trickling the liquid in slowly through the corner of his lips. Again, hold the mouth closed with the nose pointed slightly upwards, and give the cat time to swallow. This method may be used to give liquid medicines, to give some water to help a tablet go down, or even, in moderation, to get some liquidized food into a cat with no appetite.

THE ELDERLY CAT

# The Elderly Cat

▲ *A twenty-one-year-old cat enjoying his home comforts.*

THE ELDERLY CAT

The usual lifespan of a cat is about 16 or 17 years, but this varies, and it is not particularly unusual to encounter cats in their early 20s. After the age of about 14, however, a cat must be considered to be elderly. You will probably notice him slowing down gradually, spending longer periods asleep, and perhaps taking a little less care with his grooming. However, it is unusual for ageing cats to go grey in the way that humans and many dogs do. On the contrary, cats with coats of the Himalayan (Siamese) pattern, whose dark areas depend on these parts of the body (ears, nose, paws and tail) being at a rather lower temperature than the rest, frequently turn dark all over as the poorer circulation of age lowers the skin temperature as a whole.

## SPECIAL INDULGENCES

As an older cat begins to slow down, you will probably want to pamper him a little and give in to his fads more than previously. So far as food is concerned, you may find that he has become more choosy with age, and by its teens he has you well trained to produce favourite delicacies on demand. If his appetite is poor, try warming the food to around blood heat before serving to enhance the taste. Older cats tend to feel the cold more than those in the prime of life, and you will find that the provision of a heated bed is particularly appreciated, especially in winter. In addition, a less active cat may find it difficult to reach a bed situated high up on a shelf or worktop where he could leap up easily a few years before. If possible, it is best to arrange some stepping stones rather than move the bed, as older cats can be very set in their ways and resent change. Older cats are also less able to go for long periods without access to a litter tray or the garden, and if you have been in the habit of leaving your pet without a litter tray it is probably wise to introduce one indoors at this stage. Even if you have a cat flap permanently accessible, an older cat will prefer not to venture outside on a cold wet night to obey the call of nature. Sometimes an elderly cat occasionally loses control of the muscle of the anus very slightly, and passes a small amount of faeces on the carpet or in bed. It is no use scolding him for this, as it is quite involuntary, and in fact if he realizes what has happened he is likely to be very embarrassed and try to dispose of the 'accident' by eating it, before anyone else notices. A reduction in agility and an increase in indolence often cause an ageing cat to neglect its coat slightly, and in this case the maintenance of a regular grooming routine is very important. It is of course easier if the cat has been used to being groomed from kittenhood. You may also find that a proprietary fatty acid food supplement (evening primrose oil or cod-liver oil) improves the condition of a poor quality, scaly coat. This obviously also applies to nursing queens and convalescing cats.

## THE HEALTH OF THE ELDERLY CAT

As a cat grows older, general resistance to disease tends to weaken and illnesses which might have been mild a few years previously may be quite severe. It is therefore wise to ensure that booster vaccinations are kept up-to-date, especially those against cat flu. Teeth are another area of concern, as very few cats reach old age without some degree of dental or gum trouble, and this is a common reason for a poor appetite or downright refusal to eat. In most cases the treatment of dental problems will require a general anaesthetic, and so if an ageing but otherwise healthy cat has rather dubious teeth it is wise to have them attended to before health deteriorates to the point where an anaesthetic might be rather risky. Even if a cat loses most or all his teeth he will still have very little difficulty eating prepared foods, especially if the food is not served too soft but in bite-sized pieces. It is much better to be rid of teeth that are causing trouble, and you should discuss this with your vet.

Probably the commonest cause of death in an elderly cat is kidney failure, a condition which which this species is particularly prone. The earliest signs of this condition are usually excessive thirst and weight loss, but as there are many other reasons for a cat to drink a great deal, it is important to consult your vet as soon as you notice an increase in water consumption. Kidney dysfunction can best be confirmed by a blood test. There is no cure for it as such, but once the diagnosis is made your pet's life can be prolonged very significantly by the provision of a special diet and unlimited quantities of fresh water. It is most important not to restrict his drinking at all, as failing kidneys can only continue coping with body wastes if there is plenty of water available. In the later stages of kidney failure a cat may develop bad breath and mouth ulcers (but distinguish this from simple gingivitis), become very thin with a poor coat, eat very little and, finally, begin to vomit. This last is a serious sign, and often an indication that the condition has become terminal.

The other very common cause of death in old cats is neoplasia, that is, tumours of various descriptions. Symptoms will vary depending on which part of the body is affected, and include anaemia, jaundice, severe weight loss and often a very poor coat. If the tumour is in a superficial location it may be possible to see or feel a lump, but tumours in such organs as the liver will not be immediately obvious. Again, it is unlikely that any cure can be offered, and though some cases may be suitable for surgery, these conditions vary a great deal in their progress. Correct symptomatic treatment can often slow the course of the disease and give your pet many months more of comfortable life.

Chronic lung disease, liver failure and, occasionally, heart disease, are other major illnesses which may strike down an elderly cat. In many of these conditions the long-term outlook may be very poor, but you should not be afraid to take your cat to your vet for fear of a verdict of this sort. You will not be put under any pressure to have him put to sleep on the spot unless he is clearly suffering unacceptably, and early consultation can result in treatment and advice which will greatly improve the quality of your pet's final weeks or months even when the illness is ultimately terminal.

### NURSING THE TERMINALLY ILL CAT

When an illness is known to be terminal, the fundamental objective of nursing care alters. Instead of striving for cure and recovery, even if this involves some discomfort for the patient, the aim is to maintain maximum comfort and the best possible quality of life for as long as possible This inevitably involves some compromises.

You will of course want to keep your pet clean, and some extra grooming will be necessary to compensate for his own reduced care of his coat. However, you should not strive for super-high standards if this involves disturbing him too much. Eyes, nose and under the tail must of course be carefully cleaned, and dirty or very matted areas of coat attended to, but a few minor mats and grubbiness should perhaps be accepted if he seems to dislike too much grooming. You may find that your pet is unable or unwilling to move any great distance, and will often appreciate being carried to another room, a sunny spot, or the litter tray. You should, of course, make every effort to administer all treatment such as tablets or ointments exactly as prescribed by your vet. However, there may come a time when you feel that this is distressing your cat more than seems acceptable under the circumstances, and, in consultation with your vet, you may decide to reduce or discontinue treatment in order to maintain quality of life.

Feeding is an extremely important consideration. You should use every possible trick to persuade an ailing cat to eat, such as warming the food and offering favourite titbits. You may also try hand feeding, as cats will often accept food from their owner's fingers which they will not eat from a dish. Cleanliness of feeding dishes is vital, as the hint of stale food may cause the cat to turn away, and you should never leave uneaten food for long periods; instead remove it, wash the dish and provide a fresh meal. Again, you should try to adhere to your vet's advice regarding the best diet for your pet's condition, but in the final analysis it is probably more important that your cat eats something, no matter what, than sits all day staring at an untouched bowl of special precription diet. Maintenance of reasonable appetite is probably your best guide to how your pet is feeling. If he takes a reasonable amount of food, and potters quietly around the house for a short period each day, his quality of life is probably acceptable, but when an old, sick cat stops eating entirely then this is probably the time to consider the wisdom of trying to persevere much further.

### EUTHANASIA

Whatever the arguments for and against voluntary euthanasia for humans, there is no doubt that a peaceful and painless end is the last gift you can give your pet. If you are very lucky your cat may simply pass away in his sleep one night. However, it is often the case that the gradual deterioration of a degenerative disease will result in a miserable, unhappy, painful experience, and as your pet cannot understand what is happening, it is your responsibility to decide when it is the right time to end his life. Your vet will want to discuss this with you, to be sure that you are not being too hasty, or to counsel you towards enthanasia if the cat seems to be suffering unduly. You know your cat best.

A pet cat is put to sleep by the injection of an overdose of a barbiturate drug which is a commonly used anaesthetic in both animals and humans. Apart from the prick of the needle it is quite painless, and depending on just where the injection is given the cat will fall deeply asleep either immediately or within a few minutes. The sleep becomes deeper and deeper until first breathing and then the heartbeat stop. Sometimes there is a slight twitch when the heart finally stops, but there is no possibility that the cat is actually feeling anything by this stage, and it is simply a muscular reflex. You may prefer to leave your cat with the vet and depart before the deed is actually done, or you may prefer to stay to the end. Some vets very much prefer if the owner does not stay when they are putting a pet to sleep – this is usually because they themselves are somewhat upset by the sad task they have to perform and are nervous in case the cat winces slightly at the prick of the needle, or twitches towards the end, and are afraid that this might upset a watching owner. However, if you have very strong feelings about wanting to stay you should explain this to your vet, who will understand how you feel.

Your vet will be able to arrange to dispose of your pet's body for you, usually by incineration or perhaps burial. Alternatively, there are companies which operate a pet cremation service with return of the ashes, and some towns actually have pet cemeteries. If you decide to take the body home to bury it yourself then you will need to dig a grave at least four feet deep, and be sure to take precautions to protect it against digging by dogs. You should not be ashamed about feeling or showing grief for a dead pet. When a relationship has been important to you it is not healthy to suppress grief or pretend it does not exist, and it diminishes the relationship.

▲ *At thirteen years old, this cat is going a little grey around the muzzle and perhaps beginning to slow down very slightly.*

SHOWING YOUR CAT

## CHAPTER EIGHT

# Showing your Cat

▲ *The author's non-pedigree rescued stray, aged about twelve, reaches the Best in Show pen at a Championship Show.*

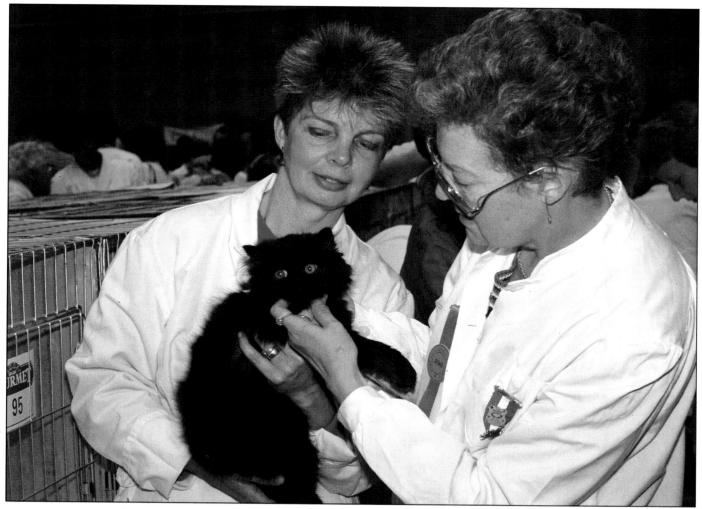

▲ *A steward holds up a black longhair for her judge to inspect at a GCCF pen-judged show.*

## WHY SHOW YOUR CAT?

For cat breeders, shows are the necessary shop window, advertising stand and marketplace for their product. The title 'Champion', or even better, 'Grand Champion', enhances a stud tom's marketability as nothing else can, and automatically improves the value of a queen and her kittens. Promising kittens may also be entered in shows as a means of attracting potential buyers. However, even if you only keep a cat as a pet, you will find that showing can be a great deal of fun. It is very satisfying to produce your pet in tip-top condition and watch him being admired by the public (and, one hopes, the judges), and shows are a marvellous place to meet other cat-mad people, exchange gossip, inspect – and perhaps buy – the latest patented cat beds, toys and so on. If you have a pedigree cat which is not perhaps in the top rank of that particular breed's standards it is still good fun to win a few small prizes at lesser shows, and even non-pedigrees are not barred from being shown. On the contrary, most shows have very popular non-pedigree ('household pet') sections in which any unregistered neutered cat may be entered,

and as judging is entirely based on condition and temperament then a kitty of the most humble origins, with a sweet nature and a shining coat, can easily go home dripping with ribbons. There are even special classes for rescued strays.

## SHOW PROCEDURE

This varies according to the organization under whose auspices the show is being held. Most countries have at least one national organization, and some have two or more, running complementary programmes. If you have not shown before, it is perhaps best to attend one show as a spectator – you will see something of what goes on, you will find people eager to give you schedules of forthcoming events, and you may be able to buy a few necessary or useful items of show equipment. When you do decide to enter your cat in its first show, it is best to choose a fairly small affair, and to save the attempts at championship shows for later. If you are showing a non-pedigree, you will find one of the exclusively non-pedigree shows which are often run as fund-raising

SHOWING YOUR CAT

▲ *Ring judging underway at the Supreme Show – note the decorated pens in the background.*

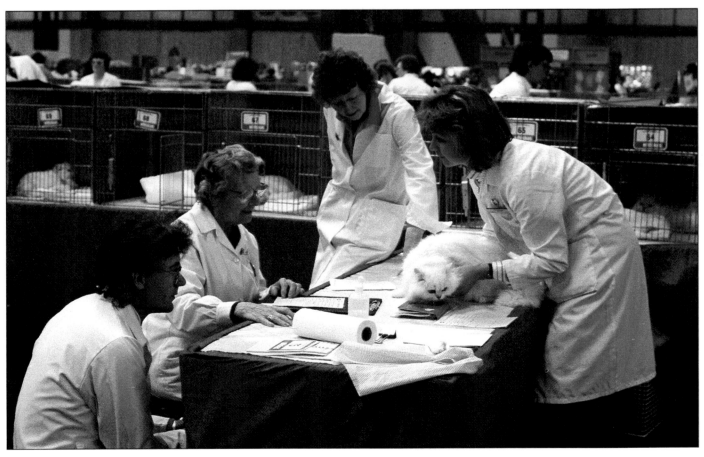

▲ *In ring judged shows the cats are brought to the judge, in this case by an army of stewards.*

▲ *This effectively decorated pen makes its occupant appear to be enjoying a 'night on the tiles'!*

events for feline charities to be an excellent starting place, as there is often a wider and more imaginative range of classes.

It is important to know the regulations governing the shows concerning veterinary inspections or how frequently you may show your cat.

### SHOWS WITH RING JUDGING

This type of procedure is adopted by the Cat Fanciers' Association (CFA) and other American associations, and the Cat Association (CA) in Britain, and is also used by the other British association, the Governing Council of the Cat Fancy (GCCF), for its supreme show. In these shows the pens in which the cats stay during the day are never seen by the judges and so may be decorated by the owners. Many attractive, amusing and intricate decorations may be seen, and there is often a special prize for the best, but simple drapes in a colour to complement your cat's coat are also very effective. The cats are taken in their baskets to rings where the judges examine them and make their selections, and at shows of this type, seating may be arranged to allow the public a good view of the judging.

■ **SHOWS WITH PEN JUDGING.** This procedure is operated by the GCCF, the main show-organizing body in Britain, for all but its supreme show. In these shows the cats remain in their own pens all day (unless eventually promoted to a 'Best in Show' pen), and the judges and their stewards move round the pens with small wheeled tables on which they examine the exhibits. In order to preserve anonymity the contents of the pen are rigidly uniform – white blanket, white litter tray, white water dish, and cat, wearing nothing but his official number on a white ribbon. It is also usual to clear the judging area while the main classes are being judged: sometimes exhibitors may watch from the sidelines or a balcony, sometimes the whole hall is cleared. However, the final judging of the winners of each main class for the 'Best in Show' titles is usually done in public.

### PREPARING FOR A SHOW

The first thing you must do is to make absolutely certain that your cat and yourself are properly registered with the body under whose auspices the show is being held. For pedigrees, your cat's breeder will be able to help you with the formalities, while the procedures for non-

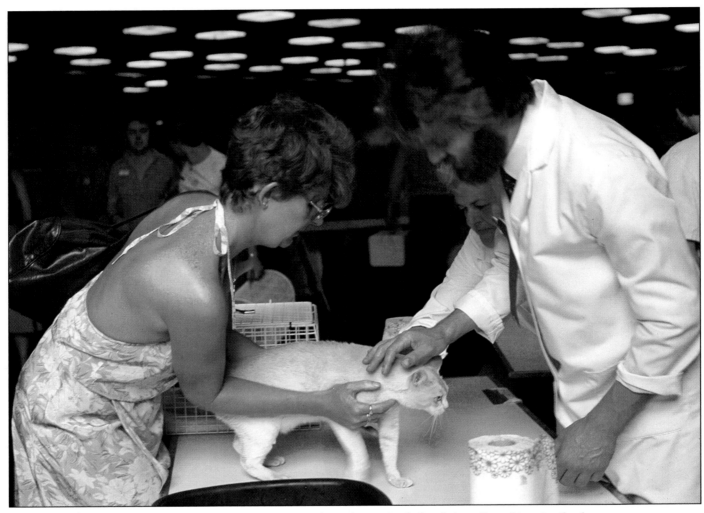

▲ *In many countries each cat must pass a veterinary inspection before being allowed to enter the show arena.*

pedigrees are usually uncomplicated, and in some organizations non-pedigrees need not be registered at all. The next thing is to acquire a schedule of classes for the show you wish to enter, in good time as the closing date for entries is usually four to six weeks before the show. It is very important to read carefully all the small print of the schedule and to follows its instructions. This will tell you which cats may not be shown (pregnant or nursing queens, toms with only one testicle, and un-neutered adult non-pedigrees, for example), which classes your cat is eligible for, what show equipment you will need (white blankets and litter tray, for example), what types of cat basket are allowed, what time you must be there for vetting-in (registration), what reasons may cause the vet to reject your cat, what time the hall must be cleared and what time you will be allowed to go home. It is also advisable to obtain a full list of show rules from the governing body, especially if you are showing a pedigree cat. Make sure your entry form is correctly filled in, and that you enclose the correct entry fee.

It is most important to accustom a potential show exhibit to being handled. Encourage competent friends and acquaintances to pick your cat up and examine him, but be careful not to put him off the whole idea by allowing rough handling or by overdoing things. Ensure he is well used to the travelling basket – if a cat can be patient and relaxed in that, then a show pen will seem quite spacious by comparison.

The nature of your cat's coat will determine how long before the show you will have to begin preparations. Persian-type longhairs require weeks of effort, often including bathing, while fine-coated shorthairs may need only the most minimal tidying up a day or two before the show. Some guidelines on general and show grooming are included in Chapter 2. On the night before a show the final grooming should be particularly thorough, including cleaning the ears, paws and under the tail. After that, make sure all necessities for the day are packed – it is useful to keep a checklist of essentials, otherwise some vital item like the can-opener or the cat litter will be forgotten. An early start is usually necessary as most shows require exhibits to be there by 9.00 or 9.30 am. Finally, once everything has been done and your cat is settled in the pen and looking his best – enjoy the show!

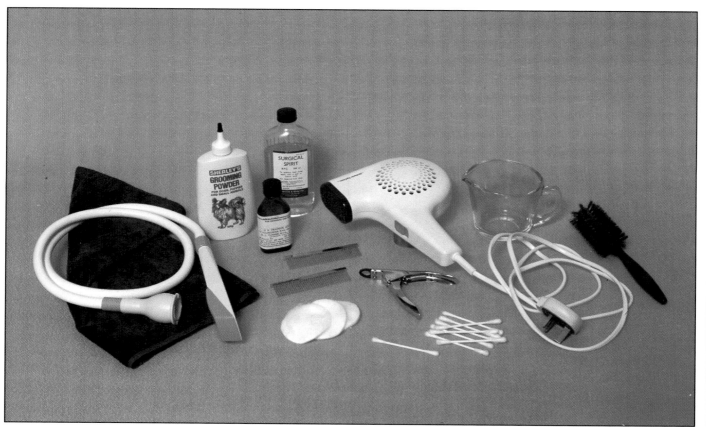

▲ *Show grooming routine for a longhair is complicated and time-consuming, and requires a lot of preparation.*

▲ *Essential equipment for a pen-judged show which is being held in cold weather. The hot water bottle is allowed so long as it is completely concealed by the white blanket.*

▲ *A cat need not have a pedigree to make a good pet or win many prizes.*

# Appendix:
# Some Popular Breeds

▲ *A Black Smoke Longhair.*

▲ *Cream Persian Longhair.*

■ **THE LONGHAIRS.** These can be very roughly divided into the Persian type (Persian, Colourpoint and Chinchilla) with cobby bodies, very short faces and very long coats; the medium longhair types (Birman, Turkish Van, Maine Coon and Ragdoll) which have longer, more wedge-shaped heads and longer bodies; and the longhair variants of certain foreign shorthair varieties (Korat, Somali, Angora and Balinese) which have fine, silky medium long coats but otherwise retain the characteristics of their shorthaired relatives.

■ **THE PERSIAN** (often referred to simply as the longhair) has a very long, dense and silky coat; a solid body with sturdy legs; and a round head with a short nose and large eyes. The breed is divided further by coat and eye colour but the basic type remains the same. Although the flat face often confers a rather sour expression these cats are frequently very docile and good-natured.

▲ *Seal-point Colourpoint Longhair.*

■ **THE COLOURPOINT** is essentially a Persian-type longhair but with the Himalayan (Siamese) coat pattern of a more deeply coloured face (mask), ears, paws and tail against a light-coloured body.

▲ *Chinchilla.*

▲ *A rare shot of a Turkish Van swimming.*

■ **THE CHINCHILLA** is again a similar type of cat, but with a white coat with a black tip to each hair giving a shimmering effect. The eyelids also have black edges, which gives a very striking kohl-rimmed appearance.

■ **THE TURKISH VAN** is again a medium longhaired breed with a long nose, and a longer body than the Persian. The colour of this breed is white with reddish-brown patchy markings. They are renowned for a liking for water and for being able to swim.

▲ *Blue Birman.*

▲ *Tortie-tabby Maine Coon.*

■ **THE BIRMAN** is not quite so extremely long-haired as the Persian, and has a more natural medium length nose. These cats also have the Himalayan coat pattern, but with the addition of white feet (gloves and gauntlets) superimposed on the coloured points.

■ **THE MAINE COON** is a semi-longhair with a medium to long nose and a long, plumed tail. In the United States this breed is renowned for its large size, however, many of the examples recently introduced into Britain have been only medium-sized cats. The name is believed to refer to the fact that the large tabby-marked individuals often look remarkably like racoons.

SOME POPULAR BREEDS

▲ *A family of seal-point Ragdolls.*

■ **THE RAGDOLL** is also a very large, semi-longhair cat, which has the unusual attribute of relaxing completely and becoming almost limp when picked up. Due to their extremely non-aggressive disposition, it is probably unwise to allow these cats to roam out of doors unsupervised.

■ **THE SOMALI** is the longhair version of the Abyssinian, but again the coat length is much shorter than that of the true longhair breeds.

▲ *Korat.*

■ **THE KORAT** is a medium to 'short' longhair type, which is otherwise very similar to the Russian Blue.

▲ *Two Angoras – a cinnamon and a blue tabby.*

■ **THE ANGORA** is an Oriental cat with a medium-long, silky, flowing coat.

▲ *Somali.*

▲ *Red-point Balinese.*

▲ *Exotic Odd-eyed White.*

■ **THE BALINESE** is the longhaired equivalent of the Siamese, but again the coat is of medium length, silky and flowing, and the cat is otherwise of Siamese type – there is no resemblance to the Colourpoint Persian.

■ **THE EXOTIC** is essentially a Persian cat with a short coat (though not quite as short as the other short-hairs).

▲ *Blue-cream (dilute tortoiseshell) British Shorthair.*

■ **THE SHORTHAIRS** These can be divided into the British- or American-type cats with a cobby body and thick, warm coat; the medium foreign varieties (Russian Blue, Abyssinian, Cornish Rex and Burmese) which are longer and slimmer cats with finer coats; and the extreme foreign type (Havana, Oriental and Siamese) which take the elongated svelte look to the ultimate.

■ **THE BRITISH OR AMERICAN SHORTHAIR** is a very solid, compact cat with fairly short legs and tail and a short, dense but quite thick coat. The head is round and the eyes large, but the nose, although short, does not have the extreme shortness of the Persian. Like the Persian, this breed is sub-divided into many different colour groupings.

▲ *Red tabby and white Manx.*

▲ *'Usual' Abyssinian (ticked or agouti coat.).*

■ **THE MANX** is essentially a British shorthair with a small hollow at the base of the spine where the tail ought to be. This is not really a separate breed, as a double helping of the Manx gene is lethal and frequent out-crossing to normal cats is necessary to avoid small litters (due to affected kittens not developing) and kittens with spina bifida.

■ **THE ABYSSINIAN** is, like the Russian, a medium foreign-build cat, with a very distinctive ticked coat produced by each hair having two or three separate bands of colour. These cats tend to be reserved and quiet in nature.

▲ *Russian Blue.*

■ **THE RUSSIAN BLUE** has a longer body, legs and tail than the preceding shorthair breeds, and its blue-grey coat is complemented by vivid green eyes.

▲ *Tortoiseshell Devon Rex.*

▲ *Red Cornish Rex.*

■ **THE CORNISH** and **DEVON REX** breeds have the longer guard hairs missing leaving only a fine, wavy undercoat. However, while the Cornish Rex is otherwise a fairly standard medium foreign build cat, the Devon Rex has a very unusual appearance (sometimes described as having pixie faces) with a short muzzle, a marked stop to the nose and large bat ears. Their whiskers are intriguingly crinkled. These cats usually have an extremely pleasant and friendly disposition, and their lack of guard hairs makes them very warm to the touch.

▲ *Chocolate Burmese.*

■ **THE BURMESE** is again of medium foreign-body type, but tending more to the Siamese extreme than the preceding breeds. They are usually of solid colour, such as brown, blue, chocolate or lilac. While they are not quite as vocal as the Siamese they are often very dominant personalities.

▲ *Chocolate Oriental Spotted Tabby.*

■ **THE ORIENTAL** is the term used to describe this same extreme foreign type of cat which comes in a non-self colour, that is, tabby or tortoiseshell.

■ **THE HAVANA** has the same solid brown colour as the Burmese, but the body type is of the extreme foreign variety, elegantly long and slim like the Siamese. Similar cats in blue, white, black, lilac and so on are simply termed 'foreign'.

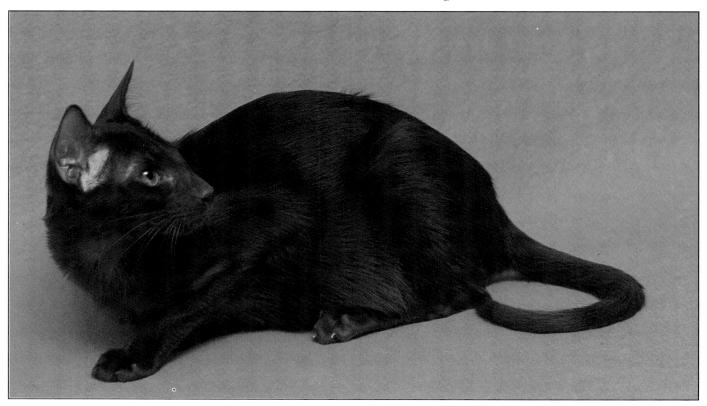

▲ *Havana Brown.*

▲ *Lilac-point Siamese.*

■ **THE SIAMESE** is the most extremely foreign of all breeds, having a long slim body, long tail and legs, and a long, wedge-shaped face. These cats all have the Himalayan coat pattern, but in a very wide variety of coloured points. The coat, like the other foreign-type cats, is extremely short and fine. Siamese have very extrovert, assertive personalities with a distinctive loud, querulous miaow which they demonstrate at every opportunity.

▲ *Classic Tabby.*

▲ *Spotted Tabby.*

■ **TABBY COAT PATTERNS.** The 'tabby' coat (the name comes from an old word for watered silk) is fundamental to feline camouflage and can be seen in nearly all very young kittens irrespective of their adult colouring. There are two basic patterns – the 'classic', with concentric rings on the flanks and three stripes along the spine, and the 'mackerel', with parallel vertical stripes on the flanks and one stripe along the spine. A variant of the latter is the 'spotted tabby' where the parallel stripes are broken into spots. For a pedigree tabby to be considered perfect, a very detailed schedule of the positions and patterns of the stripes must be adhered to exactly. Tabbies are usually brown or red (ginger), but silver and other colours are also seen, especially in pedigree cats.

---

**SUGGESTED FURTHER READING**

*The Cat Care Question and Answer Book* by Barry Bush, Orbis Publishing, 1981.
A comprehensive guide to the cat and cat care, containing answers to all the questions you wanted to ask your vet but he or she never had time to answer.
*The Silent Miaow* by Paul Gallico, Pan Books, 1964.
How to adopt and dominate a human, from the cat's point of view.

---

# Index

Figures in italics refer to picture captions.

# Picture Credits